15th Workshop on Multimodal Machine Translation for Low Resource Languages (MMTLRL 2021)

In Conjunction with the International Conference on Recent Advances in Natural Language Processing (RANLP 2021)

Online
7 September 2021

Editors:

Thoudam Doren Singh
Cristina Espana I Bonet
Sivaji Bandyopadhyay
Josef Van Genabith

ISBN: 978-1-7138-4099-2

Printed from e-media with permission by:

Curran Associates, Inc.
57 Morehouse Lane
Red Hook, NY 12571

Some format issues inherent in the e-media version may also appear in this print version.

Printed with permission by Curran Associates, Inc. (2022)

For permission requests, please contact the Association for Computational Linguistics at the address below.

Association for Computational Linguistics
209 N. Eighth Street
Stroudsburg, Pennsylvania 18360

Phone: 1-570-476-8006
Fax: 1-570-476-0860

acl@aclweb.org

Additional copies of this publication are available from:

Curran Associates, Inc.
57 Morehouse Lane
Red Hook, NY 12571 USA
Phone: 845-758-0400
Fax: 845-758-2633
Email: curran@proceedings.com
Web: www.proceedings.com

MMTLRL 2021

Proceedings
of the
First Workshop on Multimodal Machine Translation for Low Resource Languages (MMTLRL 2021)

in conjunction with

International Conference on Recent Advances in Natural Language Processing (RANLP 2021)

Edited by

Thoudam Doren Singh, Cristina España i Bonet, Sivaji Bandyopadhyay, Josef Van Genabith

September 7, 2021

Proceedings of the First Workshop on Multimodal Machine Translation for Low Resource Languages (MMTLRL 2021)
in conjunction with RANLP 2021
September 7, 2021

Preface

Language does not exist in a vacuum. Yet, for a long time, large parts of NLP have focused on text- (or speech-) only scenarios: most work on machine translation (MT) e.g. is on text-to-text MT. In principle, the inclusion of additional context in the form of other modalities offers the promise of improving a translation. In practice, this is often hard (Lala et al. 2017, Elliott 2018). In this workshop, we would like to combine two strands of research that are hitherto not well connected: research on low-resource MT and research on multi-modal MT (MMMT). The reason why we would like to explore the connection is the following: while there has been important progress on both sides, including unsupervised (Artetxe et al. 2018, Lample et al. 2018) and self-supervised MT (Ruiter et al. 2019), and neural-network based modality combinations in MMMT (Çağlayan et al. 2019), the potential of mustering information in other modalities (such as images, videos and spoken language) to complement the text signal in low-resource MT has not yet been explored extensively. However, a combination may hold promise: a richer multimodal signal may help address some of the challenges that come with low-resource scenarios. Of course, there are no guarantees: a richer multimodal signal and with it an increase in the dimensionality of the data may make the problem worse.

We acknowledge the support of this workshop under the Scheme for Promotion of Academic and Research Collaboration (SPARC) Project Code: P995 of No: SPARC/2018-2019/119/SL(IN) under Ministry of Education (erstwhile MHRD), Govt. of India. We also would like to thank Loitongbam Sanayai Meetei, Alok Singh, and Salam Michael Singh (PhD students of NIT Silchar) for their technical support.

Thoudam Doren Singh, Cristina España i Bonet, Sivaji Bandyopadhyay, Josef Van Genabith (organizers of MMTLRL 2021)

Keynote Speakers

- Marine Carpuat, University of Maryland, USA
- Lucia Specia, Imperial College London, England

Organizing Committee

- Thoudam Doren Singh, NIT Silchar, India
- Cristina España i Bonet, DFKI and Universität des Saarlandes, Germany
- Sivaji Bandyopadhyay, NIT Silchar, India
- Josef Van Genabith, DFKI and Universität des Saarlandes, Germany

Technical Programme Committee

- David Ifeoluwa Adelani, Universität des Saarlandes, Germany
- Loïc Barrault, University of Sheffield
- Pushpak Bhattacharyya, IIT Bombay, India
- Koel Dutta Chowdhury, Universität des Saarlandes, Germany
- Marta R. Costa-jussà, Universitat Politècnica de Catalunya, Spain
- Alexander Fraser, LMU Munich, Germany
- Julia Kreutzer, Google
- Gorka Labaka, University of the Basque Country (UPV/EHU), Spain
- Pranava Madhyastha, Imperial College London, England
- Vukosi Marivate, University of Pretoria, South Africa
- Loitongbam Sanayai Meetei, National Institute of Technology Silchar, India
- Preslav Nakov, Qatar Computing Research Institute, HBKU
- Shantipriya Parida, Idiap Research Institute, Switzerland
- Alok Singh, National Institute of Technology Silchar, India
- Salam Michael Singh, National Institute of Technology Silchar, India
- Xabier Soto, University of the Basque Country (UPV/EHU), Spain
- Jörg Tiedeman, University of Helsinki, Finland
- Deyi Xiong, Tianjin University, China
- Jingyi Zhang, DFKI, Germany

Table of Contents

Conference Program

6:00 *Models and Tasks for Human-Centered Machine Translation*
Marine Carpuat

7:20 *Multiple Captions Embellished Multilingual Multi-Modal Neural Machine Translation*
Salam Michael Singh, Loitongbam Sanayai Meetei, Thoudam Doren Singh and Sivaji Bandyopadhyay

7:40 *Malta National Language Technology Platform: A vision for enhancing Malta's official languages using Machine Translation*
Keith Cortis, Judie Attard and Donatienne Spiteri

7:55 *Low Resource Multimodal Neural Machine Translation of English-Hindi in News Domain*
Loitongbam Sanayai Meetei, Thoudam Doren Singh and Sivaji Bandyopadhyay

8:30 *Multimodal Simultaneous Machine Translation*
Lucia Specia

9:50 *Multimodal Neural Machine Translation System for English to Bengali*
Shantipriya Parida, Subhadarshi Panda, Satya Prakash Biswal, Ketan Kotwal, Arghyadeep Sen, Satya Ranjan Dash and Petr Motlicek

10:05 *Experiences of Adapting Multimodal Machine Translation Techniques for Hindi*
Baban Gain, Dibyanayan Bandyopadhyay and Asif Ekbal

Keynote Talk I
Models and Tasks for Human-Centered Machine Translation

Marine Carpuat
University of Maryland, USA

Abstract

In this talk, I will describe current research directions in my group that aim to make machine translation (MT) more human-centered. Instead of viewing MT solely as a task that aims to transduce a source sentence into a well-formed target language equivalent, we revisit all steps of the MT research and development lifecycle with the goal of designing MT systems that are able to help people communicate across language barriers. I will present methods to better characterize the parallel training data that powers MT systems, and how the degree of equivalence impacts translation quality. I will introduce models that enable flexible conditional language generation, and will discuss recent work on framing machine translation tasks and evaluation to center human factors.

Proceedings of the First Workshop on Multimodal Machine Translation for Low Resource Languages (MMTLRL 2021),
in conjuction with RANLP-2021, September 7, 2021. page 1
https://doi.org/10.26615/978-954-452-073-1_001

Multiple Captions Embellished Multilingual Multi-Modal Neural Machine Translation

Salam Michael Singh[1], **Loitongbam Sanayai Meetei**[1], **Thoudam Doren Singh**[1], and **Sivaji Bandyopadhyay**[1]

[1]Centre for Natural Language Processing (CNLP) & Dept. of CSE, NIT Silchar, India
{salammichaelcse,loisanayai,thoudam.doren,sivaji.cse.ju}@gmail.com

Abstract

Neural machine translation based on bilingual text with limited training data suffers from lexical diversity, which lowers the rare word translation accuracy and reduces the generalizability of the translation system. In this work, we utilise the multiple captions from the `Multi-30K` dataset to increase the lexical diversity aided with the cross-lingual transfer of information among the languages in a multilingual setup. In this multilingual and multimodal setting, the inclusion of the visual features boosts the translation quality by a significant margin. Empirical study affirms that our proposed multimodal approach achieves substantial gain in terms of the automatic score and shows robustness in handling the rare word translation in the pretext of English to/from Hindi and Telugu translation tasks.

1 Introduction

The machine translation (MT) systems by (Koehn et al., 2003; Sutskever et al., 2014; Gehring et al., 2017; Vaswani et al., 2017) has been the de-facto standard which are based on parallel dataset. But, in recent times, use of monolingual data (Singh and Singh, 2020) or incorporating multiple languages in a jointly trained single multilingual model (Johnson et al., 2017; Fan et al., 2020) has improved the translation quality of low resource languages. Compared to training separate bi-lingual models with the same parameters, the ability to handle translation between multiple language pairs provides an inherent advantage of having relatively compact model parameters. Typically, in such models, the encoder and decoders are shared among all the languages and attention. The sharing of the encoder is crucial to learn the initial multilingual cross-lingual information (Sachan and Neubig, 2018) however, a single shared decoder is often insufficient in handling the translation of multiple languages. This decoder degeneracy is addressed by partial sharing of decoder and attention parameters (Sachan and Neubig, 2018) or through a language-agnostic universal models (Bapna and Firat, 2019).

Image features along with the text data has been used in sequence generation tasks such as the image caption generation (Singh et al., 2021a,b) and multimodal machine translation (MMT) which incorporates visual features into ordinary NMT systems for low resource languages. With the introduction of MMT datasets such as `Multi-30k` (Elliott et al., 2016) and Hindi Visual Genome Parida et al. (2019), MT researchers (Huang et al., 2016; Caglayan et al., 2016, 2019; Meetei et al., 2019) have highlighted improvement in translation quality by incorporating image features in the MT systems.

In this work, we adopt a single shared multilingual machine translation system between English and under resourced languages viz., Hindi and Telugu, aided by linguistic information in the form of multiple captions. The inclusion of multiple captions during training makes the system implicitly robust to lexical and syntactic diversity. In addition to the multiple captions, we infuse our multi-caption multilingual model with the visual information in a multimodal (Calixto et al., 2017a; Elliott and Kádár, 2017; Yao and Wan, 2020) setting. English and Hindi belong to the Indo-European language family, while Telugu is a Dravidian language. All three languages use different scripts; Roman for English, Devanagari for Hindi and Telugu is written in Telugu script, an abugida writing system from the Brahmic family of scripts.

2 Related Works

Callison-Burch et al. (2006) used paraphrase in a phrase-based statistical machine translation model

Proceedings of the First Workshop on Multimodal Machine Translation for Low Resource Languages (MMTLRL 2021), in conjuction with RANLP-2021, September 7, 2021. pages 2–11
https://doi.org/10.26615/978-954-452-073-1_002

and found that their method improves over the single parallel corpora PB-SMT baseline in terms of the overall word coverage and the translation quality. Paraphrase has also been leveraged as a data augmentation technique to improve dialog generation (Gao et al., 2020) and question generation (Jia et al., 2020) tasks. More similar to our proposed work Zhou et al. (2019) decomposed the paraphrase as a foreign language in a multilingual scenario. Similar to the findings of Callison-Burch et al. (2006), Zhou et al. (2019) found that their method improves the word coverage with diverse lexical choices.

However, these works are purely uni-modal, and on the other hand, a visually informed multimodal system involves the extraction of the global semantic features from the image and initialize either the encoder or decoder to fuse the visual context along with the textual input (Calixto et al., 2017b). In cases where the textual context is restricted, Caglayan et al. (2019) showed that visual features could help to generate better translations. Similar to the proposed work, (Chakravarthi et al., 2019) trained a multimodal machine translation system in the pretext of Tamil, Kannada and Malayalam by generating a synthetic dataset from Flickr30k (Plummer et al., 2015). They showed that transliteration of the Dravidian languages into Latin script and the multilingual setup improves the multimodal system over the bilingual multimodal baseline.

3 Methodology

The proposed multi-caption enabled multi-modal multilingual machine translation system employs two major steps: first, we create the training corpus and then train the multi-caption multilingual system fused with the visual features.

3.1 Corpus Creation

The creation of a training corpus for the experimentation is the first step. Multilingual machine translation with visual features for English (*en*) to/from {Hindi (*hi*), Telugu (*te*)} is the experiment's premise. `Multi-30K` (Elliott et al., 2016), on the other hand, lacks the *hi* and *te* data. As a result, for training, validation, and test data, a publicly available machine translation model (Ramesh et al., 2021) generates the *hi* and *te* translations corresponding to the English captions[1] (`caption-1` and `caption-2`).

[1]Further details are provided in the Dataset section.

Initially, all the `caption-1` instances are suffixed with the *prefix.lang1* while *prefix.lang2* for the `caption-2` where *prefix* $\in$ (train, validation, test) and *lang* $\in$ (*en*, *hi*, *te*). Furthermore, during the many-to-one (**m2o**) training, all the *en* instances of the train and validation are merged into a single compound target language while all the non-English instances are merged as the source language. Here, we do not append any artificial target token at the source side to denote the target language as English is the sole target language. On the other hand, for the one-to-many (**o2m**) training all the *en* instances of the train and validation are merged into as the source language while all the non-English instances are merged as the target language. In this case, an artificial target language token <__*tgt*__*lang*> is appended at the beginning of the source sentence to denote the target language *lang* $\in$ (*hi1*, *te1*, *hi2*, *te2*).

3.2 Neural Machine Translation (NMT)

NMT is an encoder-decoder based sequence-to-sequence approach to machine translation which jointly models the conditional probability $p(\mathbf{y}|\mathbf{x})$ to translate a target sequence, $\mathbf{y} = \{y_1, \ldots, y_m\}$ given a source sequence, $\mathbf{x} = \{x_1, \ldots, x_n\}$ as:

$$p(\mathbf{y}|\mathbf{x};\theta) = \prod_{j=1}^{m} p(y_j|\mathbf{y}_{<j}, \mathbf{x}; \theta),$$

where θ is the set of learnable model parameters. Furthermore, the model objective is to maximize the log-likelihood $\mathcal{L}$ w.r.t θ by the following equation:

$$\mathcal{L}_\theta = \sum_{(\mathbf{x},\mathbf{y})\in\mathcal{D}} log\ p(\mathbf{y}|\mathbf{x};\theta), \quad (1)$$

where $\mathcal{D}$ is the parallel corpus. RNN (Sutskever et al., 2014; Bahdanau et al., 2014; Luong et al., 2015), CNN (Gehring et al., 2017) and Transformers (Vaswani et al., 2017) are the popular choice of encoder-decoder models. In this work, we use RNN with cross attention between the encoder and the decoder.

3.3 Multilingual NMT (MNMT)

Multilingual NMT facilitates the translation between multiple languages via pivot based (Dabre et al., 2015), transfer learning (Zoph et al., 2016) or through a jointly trained single NMT model (Johnson et al., 2017). In this work, we utilise the jointly trained single multilingual NMT model. Additionally, this single MNMT can be further divided into three types according to the mapping of the source and the target languages:

1. **Many-to-one (m2o)**. In this setting, the model is trained to translate multiple source languages into a single target language.

2. **One-to-many (o2m)**. This MNMT model translates from a single source language to multiple target languages.

3. **Many-to-many (m2m)**. Here, translation between many source and many target languages is possible.

Moreover, as there are several target languages in the **o2m** and **m2m**, a target language tag is appended at the beginning of the source sentence to specify the predicted target language. Given K sentence pairs and L language pairs the training objective of an MNMT model is to maximise the log-likelihood over the whole parallel pairs $\{\mathbf{x}^{(l,k)}, \mathbf{y}^{(l,k)}\}_{k\in(1,\ldots,K_l)}^{l\in(1,\ldots,L)}$ as:

$$\mathcal{L}_\theta = \frac{1}{K}\sum_{l=1}^{L}\sum_{k=1}^{K_l} log\ p(\mathbf{y}^{(l,k)}|\mathbf{x}^{(l,k)};\theta), \quad (2)$$

where the total parallel sentences $K = \sum_{l=1}^{L} K_l$.

3.4 Multimodal Machine Translation (MMT)

We follow the Calixto et al. (2017a) MMT model, an expansion of the attention-based NMT framework (Bahdanau et al., 2014), where visual features are incorporated. Spatial features extracted from the image using pre-trained CNNs are incorporated with an attention mechanism in the decoder. When generating the target words, the model learns to independently input textual and visual context using separate attention mechanisms in a single decoder RNN. The decoder RNN is conditioned on the image, source sentence, previous hidden state, and previously emitted words through an independent attention mechanism. Given a new multimodal hidden state $\mathbf{s}_j$, the previous emitted word $\mathbf{y}_{<j}$, context vector $\mathbf{c}_j$ from encoder source sentence and context vector $\boldsymbol{i}_j$ from image features, the decoder computes a new probability to generate a target word using Equation 3.

$$\begin{aligned} p(y_j = k|\mathbf{y}_{<j}, C, A) = softmax(\boldsymbol{L}_o tanh(\\ \boldsymbol{L}_s\mathbf{s}_j + \boldsymbol{L}_w\boldsymbol{E}_y[y_{j-1}]\boldsymbol{L}_{cs}\mathbf{c}_j + \boldsymbol{L}_{ci}\boldsymbol{i}_j)) \end{aligned} \quad (3)$$

where $\boldsymbol{L}_o$, $\boldsymbol{L}_s$, $\boldsymbol{L}_w$, $\boldsymbol{L}_{cs}$, and $\boldsymbol{L}_{ci}$ are projection matrices.

3.5 Multilingual Multimodal MT (M2MT) with Multiple Captions (MC)

Using the multilingual multi-caption augmented corpus discussed in Section 3.1, a multi-modal machine translation model is trained in **o2m** and **m2o** fashion. Both the visual information fused **o2m** and **m2o** models are trained by maximizing the following log-likelihood:

$$\mathcal{L}_\theta = \frac{1}{K}\sum_{l=1}^{L}\sum_{k=1}^{K_l} log\ p(\mathbf{y}^{(l,k)}|\mathbf{x}^{(l,k)}, \boldsymbol{i}^k;\theta), \quad (4)$$

where $\boldsymbol{i}^k$ is the image feature corresponding to the kth caption.

4 Experimental setup

4.1 Dataset

In this work, we use the `Multi-30K` (Elliott et al., 2016) corpus. Specifically, the first two caption descriptions (`caption-1` and `caption-2`) of *task2*[2] are used and evaluated upon the `test_2016` test set. Since our work is the multilingual machine translation for *en* to/from {*hi*,*te*}, we use a publicly available pre-trained machine translation model (Ramesh et al., 2021) to translate the English data of the `Multi-30K` to *hi* and *te*, which is further used as the parallel corpus for our experimentation.

During the evaluation process, we use the `caption-1` instance of the test set only.

4.1.1 Text Preprocessing

The text preprocessing step initially tokenizes the raw texts. English side data is tokenized using the *moses-scripts*[3] while the *hi* and *te* data are normalized and tokenized using the `IndicNLP` toolkit[4]. Additionally, the *te* side data is transliterated into Devanagari script (the same script as the *hi*). Finally, sentencepiece (Kudo and Richardson, 2018) BPE (Sennrich et al., 2016) of 10,000 subword merge operations is learnt across all the training data jointly from both the captions to increase the vocabulary coverage. The transliteration of *te* into the *hi* script further maximises the common

[2] `https://github.com/multi30k/dataset/tree/master/data/task2`

[3] `https://github.com/moses-smt/mosesdecoder/tree/master/scripts`

[4] `https://github.com/anoopkunchukuttan/indic_nlp_library`

word/subword overlaps even with smaller vocabulary size. Furthermore, using a common script prevents subword vocabulary fragmentation between the *hi* and *te* and improves lexical sharing among the languages (Ramesh et al., 2021). We use the same vocabulary throughout the experimentation.

4.2 Training Settings

NMT System: We use attention (Luong et al., 2015) based LSTM (Hochreiter and Schmidhuber, 1997) having 2 layers encoder-decoder network with 500 word embedding vector and hidden vector size. Stochastic Gradient Descent is used to optimise the training, which is trained for a maximum of 200,000 update steps, validated after every 10,000 update steps, and halted after 10 consecutive stalls in the validation perplexity. During the decoding time, the <UNK> tokens are replaced by a source word with the highest alignment score, and the translation is generated using beam search (Tillmann and Ney, 2003) with a beam size of 5. Finally, the training is done on `OpenNMT-Py` (Klein et al., 2017).

MMT System: The MMT system is trained by incorporating the image features extracted using a VGG19-CNN pre-trained model and the processed text with a batch size of 64 until validation perplexity doesn't improve for 10 consecutive epochs. A bidirectional LSTM encoder with 2 layers and a dropout with a probability of 0.2 in both source and target word embeddings is used.

4.3 Baselines

We compare our approach with the following baselines:

1. **Single caption bilingual models (NMT).** The first baseline is the four bilingual models, i.e. *en-hi*, *en-te*, *hi-en* and *te-en* trained only on `caption-1`.

2. **Multiple caption bilingual models (NMT+MC).** The second baseline is the four bilingual models trained on both `caption-1` and `caption-2`.

3. **Single caption text only multilingual models (MNMT).** The third baseline is the two multilingual models (**m2o** and **o2m**) trained on `caption-1` only.

4. **Multiple caption text only multilingual models (MNMT+MC).** Multilingual models (**m2o** and **o2m**) jointly trained on both the captions.

5. **Single caption multilingual multimodal models (M2MT).** Multilingual models (**m2o** and **o2m**) trained on `caption-1` only along with the visual features.

4.4 Evaluation

The systems are evaluated using both the automatic and human evaluation approach.

4.4.1 Automatic Evaluation

To report the automatic evaluation score, we use the BLEU (Papineni et al., 2002) and chrF both computed using the SacreBLEU (Post, 2018) implementation.

1. **BLEU**: The BLEU score is reported over the geometric mean of the 4-gram precision or BLEU-4, ranging from 0-100, with 100 being the highest. The hypothesis is detokenized and then retokenized using SacreBLEU's inbuilt mteval-13a tokenizer[5] for the Indic to English evaluation. Meanwhile, for the English to Indic translation evaluation, the hypothesis is detokenized and then retokenized using the IndicNLP tokenizer and then evaluated without using any tokenizer in SacreBLEU[6]. Furthermore, the Telugu translation is transliterated back to the Telugu script for the assessment.

2. **chrF**: The processing step for reporting the evaluation score of the chrF[7] is similar to that of the BLEU. Additionally, the chrF score scales from 0-1, where the perfect translation gets a score of 1.

4.4.2 Human Evaluation

Human evaluation is carried out by considering the fluency and adequacy of the translated output. In this pretext, a human translator fluent in English and Hindi is assigned to separately rate each sentence from 1-5 for the fluency and the adequacy criteria. Finally, the sentence wise scores are averaged to get the corpus level score for both the criteria.

[5] BLEU+case.mixed+numrefs.1+smooth.exp+tok.13a+version.1.5.1
[6] BLEU+case.mixed+numrefs.1+smooth.exp+tok.none+version.1.5.1
[7] chrF2+numchars.6+space.false+version.1.5.1

Systems	*en-hi*		*hi-en*		*en-te*		*te-en*	
	BLEU-4	chrF	BLEU-4	chrF	BLEU-4	chrF	BLEU-4	chrF
NMT-full	35.3	0.52	38.9	0.57	27	0.56	38.8	0.58
MNMT-full	48.6	0.62	47	0.65	31.2	0.59	41.1	0.6
M2MT-full	54.4	0.7	55.1	0.72	37.8	0.66	48.3	0.67

Table 1: Overall scores of the systems

Systems	*en-hi*	*hi-en*	*en-te*	*te-en*
NMT	33.2	34.5	24.9	31.3
NMT + MC	35.3	38.9	27	38.8
MNMT	45.5	43.6	29	36.4
MNMT + MC	48.6	47	31.2	41.1
MNMT + V (M2MT)	51.9	53.3	35	46.1
MNMT + V + MC (M2MT + MC)	**54.4**	**55.1**	**37.8**	**48.3**

Table 2: Ablation study of the systems based on the BLEU-4 scores.

5 Results and Analysis

This section presents the quantitative results obtained by all the models and their analysis.

5.1 Overall Result of the Automatic Evaluation

Table 1 compares the overall scores of the proposed multimodal system (M2MT-full) to the bilingual (NMT-full) and multilingual (MNMT-full) baseline variants in terms of BLEU-4 and chrF scores. M2MT-full significantly improves in BLEU and chrF scores over the NMT-full and MNMT-full baselines, with +19.1, +5.8 BLEU and +0.18, +0.08 chrF improvements for the *en-hi* translation, +16.2, +8.1 BLEU and +0.15, +0.07 chrf improvements for the *hi-en* translation. Similarly, +10.8, +6.6 BLEU and +0.1, +0.07 chrf improvements for the *en-te* translation. And, +9.5, +7.2 BLEU and +0.09, +0.07 chrf improvements for the *te-en* translation.

5.2 Ablation Study

Table 2 summarises the ablation study and quantifies the contribution of the components, namely multilinguality, multiple captions (MC), and visual features (V).

1. **Effect of the multiple languages**: In Table 2, the multilingual system (MNMT) achieves a substantial gain over the bilingual system (NMT) in BLEU scores for all translation directions. The *en-hi* translation benefits the most from the MNMT with a +12.3 BLEU improvement over the NMT followed by *hi-en* translation with +9.1 increment. Hence for this dataset, the multilinguality is effective for all the translation directions and more prominent when *hi* language is involved. This substantial gain in BLEU score in the multilingual setting can be credited to the cross-lingual information shared between Hindi and Telugu. Furthermore, the transliteration of Telugu into the Hindi script maximizes the subword overlapping during the vocabulary buildup, thus increasing the word coverage of the model as a whole. We illustrate the word coverage in the form of rare word translation accuracy in Section 5.4.
2. **Effect of the multiple captions**: We utilise the multiple captions (**MC**) provided in the `Multi-30K` dataset in our models. In doing so, a substantial gain in the BLEU score is observed when multiple captions are added over the single caption models for all the translation directions. We hypothesize that the multiple captions increase the models' generalizability by imposing a lexical enhancement as it introduces diverse word forms for the same context. Further, the increase in lexical choice makes the system more robust in handling the rare word translation.
3. **Effect of the visual features**: The addition of the visual features to the MNMT system further outperforms all the text only models even without the inclusion of the multiple captions. Furthermore, the translation accuracy of the

Systems	Adequacy	Fluency
NMT	1.85	2.95
NMT + MC	2.1	3
MNMT	2.65	2.95
MNMT + MC	3	2.85
M2MT	3.15	3.05
M2MT + MC	3.2	3.55

Table 3: Human evaluation of the systems for English to Hindi translation.

words based on their frequency in the training corpus, which we discuss in Section 5.4, reveals that visual features are beneficial for handling the rare word translation.

5.2.1 Human Evaluation Results

Apart from the automatic scores reported in Table 1 and Table 2, human evaluation result for the English to Hindi translation of all the systems is also reported in Table 3. The evaluation is conducted based the fluency and adequacy criteria. As such, both the human evaluation and the automatic scores correlates well suggesting the effectiveness of the proposed method. However, the highest adequacy and fluency scores (3.2 and 3.55 of **M2MT+MC**) is far lesser than the upper limit of the scores (a score of 5). On the other hand, the automatic scores are relatively higher. This is due to training the systems on the synthetic data as only the English side training data is real, as a result the errors in the training data are accumulated to the translated outputs. However, the human evaluator catches these errors and hence the low adequacy and fluency scores.

5.3 Qualitative Analysis

We also present the qualitative analysis of the models based on the translation outputs. In doing so, we use certain abbreviations for the readability purpose of the non-English sentences: TT is the English transliteration, Gloss denotes the word-to-word English translation, and ET denotes the English translation for the same. Moreover, texts are also colour coded based on the similarity/dissimilarity of the translation with the reference. Blue colour depicts the exact match between the reference and the translation. Meanwhile, cyan and red are errors with red denoting wrong translation and the outputs with good translation but absent in reference is denoted by cyan. The first source sentence (**English Source**) in Figure 4 presents the English to Hindi translations while the second source sentence (**Hindi Source**) illustrates the Hindi to English translations of the models.

In Figure 4 for the English to Hindi translation, both the bilingual variants wrongly generates the phrases "peeth karate hain" (with their backs) by the **NMT** and "kaimare ke saath daudate hain" (run with the camera) by the **NMT+MC** which is highlighted in red color, thus changing the actual meaning of the source sentence. Additionally, the **M2MT** system generates "yaard" (yard) instead of the "maidaan" (field) as in the reference, which is technically correct but penalised by the automatic score. Finally, **M2MT+MC** is the only system to generate the correct determiner "ek" (a). Apart from these, all the system outputs follow the subject-object-verb (SOV) word order of the target language (Hindi), irrespective of preserving the actual context of the reference. However, there are cases of interchanging the present continuous tense to simple present tense form such as generation of "daudate hain" (run) instead of "daud rahe hain" (running) as in the reference. In this regard, **MNMT**, **M2MT** and **M2MT+MC** systems produce the correct generation.

On the other hand, the Hindi to English translation presented in Figure 4 highlights the effectiveness of the multiple captions (MC) by maximizing the coverage of the reference words in the output, thus making the translation more adequate. Additionally, it is observed that except for the **MNMT+MC** all other systems wrongly generates the pronoun "his" instead of "its", which further highlights the gender biasedness of the systems. However, the translated output of **M2MT+MC** covers most of the reference words. It is syntactically correct (apart from the wrong pronoun "his"), thus making the translation more adequate and fluent than the outputs of the other baselines.

5.4 Error Analysis

We conduct the error analysis of the systems considering the translation accuracy of the words based on their frequency in the training corpus, which is illustrated in Figure 1. The translation accuracy provides an insight into the word coverage and how well the system handles the translation of rare words. The proposed multimodal system **M2MT+MC** improves the translation accuracy for the entire vocabulary and the rare words to the training corpus in particular. The **NMT**

Input Image	Model Outputs
 *en-hi* Translation	**English Source:** Three little children in a grassy yard running towards the camera. **Reference:** एक घास के मैदान में तीन छोटे बच्चे कैमरे की ओर दौड़ रहे हैं। TT: ek ghaas ke maidaan mein teen chhote bachche kaimare kee or daud rahe hain. Gloss: one grass's field in three little children camera towards running. ET: Three little children are running towards the camera in a grassy field. **NMT:** घास में तीन छोटे बच्चे कैमरे की ओर पीठ करते हैं। TT: ghaas mein teen chhote bachche kaimare kee or peeth karate hain. Gloss: grass in three little children camera towards back do. ET: Three little children in the grass with their backs to the camera. **NMT+MC:** घास के मैदान में तीन छोटे बच्चे कैमरे के साथ दौड़ते हैं। TT: ghaas ke maidaan mein teen chhote bachche kaimare ke saath daudate hain. Gloss: grass's field in three little children camera with run. ET: Three little children run with the camera in the grassy field. **MNMT:** घास के मैदान में तीन छोटे बच्चे कैमरे की ओर दौड़ रहे हैं। TT: ghaas ke maidaan mein teen chhote bachche kaimare kee or daud rahe hain. Gloss: grass's field in three little children camera towards running. ET: Three little children are running towards the camera in the grass field. **MNMT+MC:** घास के मैदान में तीन छोटे बच्चे कैमरे की ओर दौड़ते हैं। TT: ghaas ke maidaan mein teen chhote bachche kaimare kee or daudate hain. Gloss: grass's field in three little children camera towards run. ET: Three little children run towards the camera in the grassy field. **M2MT:** घास के यार्ड में तीन छोटे बच्चे कैमरे की ओर दौड़ रहे हैं। TT: ghaas ke yaard mein teen chhote bachche kaimare kee or daud rahe hain. Gloss: grass's yard in three little children camera camera towards running. ET: Three little children are running towards the camera in the grassy yard. **M2MT+MC:** घास के एक मैदान में तीन छोटे बच्चे कैमरे की ओर दौड़ रहे हैं। TT: ghaas ke ek maidaan mein teen chhote bachche kaimare kee or daud rahe hain. Gloss: grass's one field in three little children camera camera towards running. ET: Three little children are running towards the camera in a grassy field.
 *hi-en* Translation	**Hindi Source**: भूरे रंग का कुत्ता अपने दांतों के साथ दूसरे कुत्ते के गाल पर पकड़ रखता है। TT: bhoore rang ka kutta apane daanton ke saath doosare kutte ke gaal par pakad rakhata hai. Gloss: brown colour's dog its teeth with other dogs cheeks on holds. ET: The brown dog holds the other dog's cheek with its teeth. **Reference**: The brown dog has a hold of the other dogs cheek with its teeth. **NMT:** The brown dog is holding the other dog on the other dog with his teeth. **NMT+MC:** The brown dog has his teeth on the cheek of the other dog. **MNMT:** The brown dog holds on the cheek of his teeth with his teeth. **MNMT+MC:** The brown dog holds on to another dog with its teeth. **M2MT:** The brown dog grabs the other dog with his teeth on the cheek. **M2MT+MC:** The brown dog holds on to the cheek of another dog with his teeth.

Table 4: Sample input and output for the *en-hi* translation.

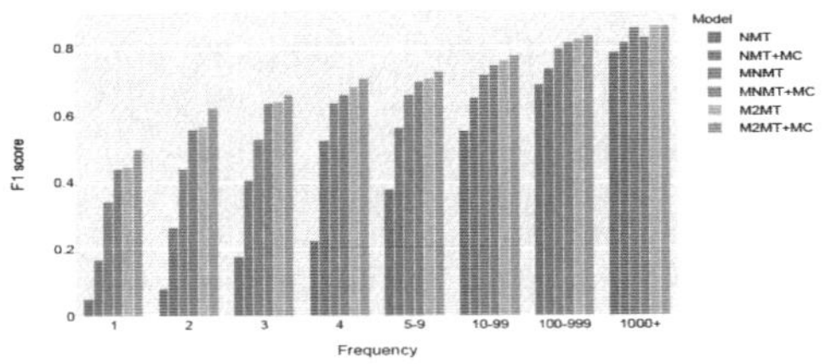

(a) *en-hi*

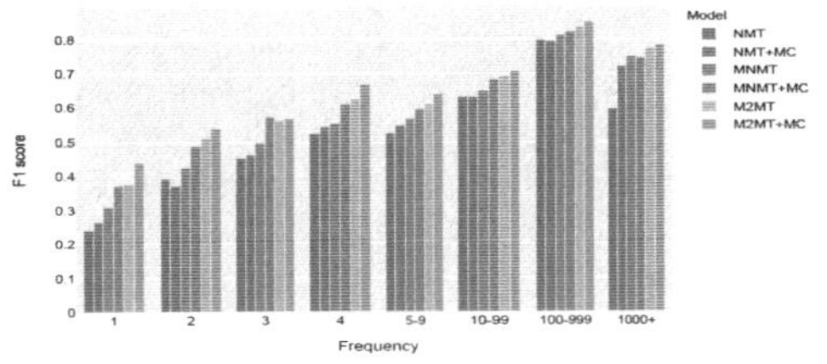

(b) *en-te*

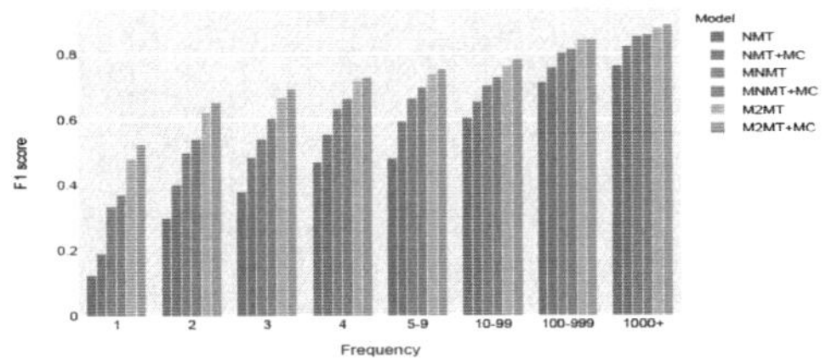

(c) *hi-en*

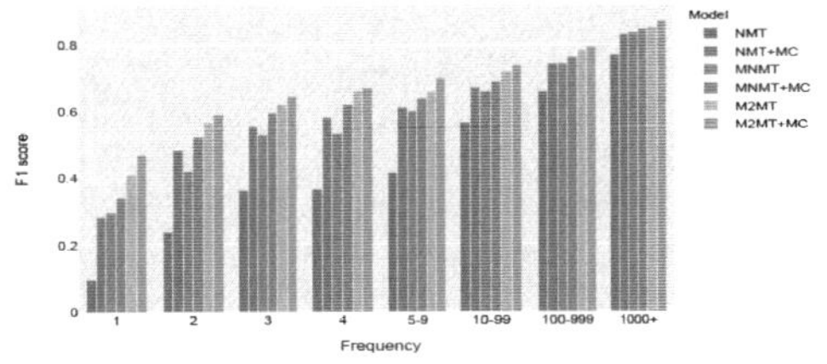

(d) *te-en*

Figure 1: F1 accuracy of target word translation based on the word frequency in the training corpus.

without any embellishments lags behind the accuracy of **NMT+MC** for the rare word translation. Similarly, the performance of all other model variants degrades when the multiple captions are not included and further strengthens the role of **MC** in the improvement of the translation quality as a whole. Additionally, the multilingual system (**MNMT**) has higher accuracy for rare word translation than both the bilingual variants (**NMT** and **NMT+MC**) for all translation directions. However for the *te-en* translation, **NMT+MC** gives a competitive performance with **MNMT** for the rarest word and sometimes better for relatively frequent words.

6 Conclusion

This work presents the multimodal machine translation embellished with multiple captions in a multilingual setup. We find that the multiple captions benefit both the text-only and the multimodal models by introducing lexical diversity, making the system more robust to handle the rare word translation and thus increasing the translation quality. Additionally, the visual features which provide the context information further alleviate the translation quality. However, this work is experimented on synthetic data, hence the trained systems possesses the accumulated errors present in the training data. In our future work, we intend to address this issue with some counter measures.

Acknowledgments

This work is supported by Scheme for Promotion of Academic and Research Collaboration (SPARC) Project Code: P995 of No: SPARC/2018-2019/119/SL(IN) under Ministry of Education (erstwhile MHRD), Govt. of India. The authors would like to thank the anonymous reviewers for providing critical suggestions. The authors also thank the volunteers for their help in human evaluation tasks.

References

Dzmitry Bahdanau, Kyunghyun Cho, and Yoshua Bengio. 2014. Neural machine translation by jointly learning to align and translate. *arXiv preprint arXiv:1409.0473*.

Ankur Bapna and Orhan Firat. 2019. Simple, scalable adaptation for neural machine translation. In *Proceedings of the 2019 Conference on Empirical Methods in Natural Language Processing and the 9th International Joint Conference on Natural Language Processing (EMNLP-IJCNLP)*, pages 1538–

1548, Hong Kong, China. Association for Computational Linguistics.

Ozan Caglayan, Walid Aransa, Yaxing Wang, Marc Masana, Mercedes García-Martínez, Fethi Bougares, Loïc Barrault, and Joost Van de Weijer. 2016. Does multimodality help human and machine for translation and image captioning? *arXiv preprint arXiv:1605.09186*.

Ozan Caglayan, Pranava Madhyastha, Lucia Specia, and Loïc Barrault. 2019. Probing the need for visual context in multimodal machine translation. *arXiv preprint arXiv:1903.08678*.

Iacer Calixto, Qun Liu, and Nick Campbell. 2017a. Doubly-attentive decoder for multi-modal neural machine translation. In *Proceedings of the 55th Annual Meeting of the Association for Computational Linguistics (Volume 1: Long Papers)*, pages 1913–1924, Vancouver, Canada. Association for Computational Linguistics.

Iacer Calixto, Qun Liu, and Nick Campbell. 2017b. Incorporating global visual features into attention-based neural machine translation. *arXiv preprint arXiv:1701.06521*.

Chris Callison-Burch, Philipp Koehn, and Miles Osborne. 2006. Improved statistical machine translation using paraphrases. In *Proceedings of the Human Language Technology Conference of the NAACL, Main Conference*, pages 17–24, New York City, USA. Association for Computational Linguistics.

Bharathi Raja Chakravarthi, Ruba Priyadharshini, Bernardo Stearns, Arun Jayapal, Sridevy S, Mihael Arcan, Manel Zarrouk, and John P McCrae. 2019. Multilingual multimodal machine translation for Dravidian languages utilizing phonetic transcription. In *Proceedings of the 2nd Workshop on Technologies for MT of Low Resource Languages*, pages 56–63, Dublin, Ireland. European Association for Machine Translation.

Raj Dabre, Chenhui Chu, Fabien Cromieres, Toshiaki Nakazawa, and Sadao Kurohashi. 2015. Large-scale dictionary construction via pivot-based statistical machine translation with significance pruning and neural network features. In *Proceedings of the 29th Pacific Asia Conference on Language, Information and Computation*, pages 289–297, Shanghai, China.

Desmond Elliott, Stella Frank, Khalil Sima'an, and Lucia Specia. 2016. Multi30K: Multilingual English-German image descriptions. In *Proceedings of the 5th Workshop on Vision and Language*, pages 70–74, Berlin, Germany. Association for Computational Linguistics.

Desmond Elliott and Ákos Kádár. 2017. Imagination improves multimodal translation. In *Proceedings of the Eighth International Joint Conference on Natural Language Processing (Volume 1: Long Papers)*, pages 130–141, Taipei, Taiwan. Asian Federation of Natural Language Processing.

Angela Fan, Shruti Bhosale, Holger Schwenk, Zhiyi Ma, Ahmed El-Kishky, Siddharth Goyal, Mandeep Baines, Onur Çelebi, Guillaume Wenzek, Vishrav Chaudhary, Naman Goyal, Tom Birch, Vitaliy Liptchinsky, Sergey Edunov, Edouard Grave, Michael Auli, and Armand Joulin. 2020. Beyond english-centric multilingual machine translation. *ArXiv*, abs/2010.11125.

Silin Gao, Yichi Zhang, Zhijian Ou, and Zhou Yu. 2020. Paraphrase augmented task-oriented dialog generation. In *Proceedings of the 58th Annual Meeting of the Association for Computational Linguistics*, pages 639–649, Online. Association for Computational Linguistics.

Jonas Gehring, Michael Auli, David Grangier, and Yann Dauphin. 2017. A convolutional encoder model for neural machine translation. In *Proceedings of the 55th Annual Meeting of the Association for Computational Linguistics (Volume 1: Long Papers)*, pages 123–135, Vancouver, Canada. Association for Computational Linguistics.

Sepp Hochreiter and Jürgen Schmidhuber. 1997. Long short-term memory. *Neural Computation*, 9(8):1735–1780.

Po-Yao Huang, Frederick Liu, Sz-Rung Shiang, Jean Oh, and Chris Dyer. 2016. Attention-based multimodal neural machine translation. In *Proceedings of the First Conference on Machine Translation: Volume 2, Shared Task Papers*, pages 639–645.

Xin Jia, Wenjie Zhou, Xu Sun, and Yunfang Wu. 2020. How to ask good questions? try to leverage paraphrases. In *Proceedings of the 58th Annual Meeting of the Association for Computational Linguistics*, pages 6130–6140, Online. Association for Computational Linguistics.

Melvin Johnson, Mike Schuster, Quoc V. Le, Maxim Krikun, Yonghui Wu, Zhifeng Chen, Nikhil Thorat, Fernanda Viégas, Martin Wattenberg, Greg Corrado, Macduff Hughes, and Jeffrey Dean. 2017. Google's multilingual neural machine translation system: Enabling zero-shot translation. *Transactions of the Association for Computational Linguistics*, 5:339–351.

Guillaume Klein, Yoon Kim, Yuntian Deng, Jean Senellart, and Alexander Rush. 2017. OpenNMT: Open-source toolkit for neural machine translation. In *Proceedings of ACL 2017, System Demonstrations*, pages 67–72, Vancouver, Canada. Association for Computational Linguistics.

Philipp Koehn, Franz J. Och, and Daniel Marcu. 2003. Statistical phrase-based translation. In *Proceedings of the 2003 Human Language Technology Conference of the North American Chapter of the Association for Computational Linguistics*, pages 127–133.

Taku Kudo and John Richardson. 2018. SentencePiece: A simple and language independent subword tokenizer and detokenizer for neural text processing. In *Proceedings of the 2018 Conference on Empirical Methods in Natural Language Processing: System Demonstrations*, pages 66–71, Brussels, Belgium. Association for Computational Linguistics.

Thang Luong, Hieu Pham, and Christopher D. Manning. 2015. Effective approaches to attention-based neural machine translation. In *Proceedings of the 2015 Conference on Empirical Methods in Natural Language Processing*, pages 1412–1421, Lisbon, Portugal. Association for Computational Linguistics.

Loitongbam Sanayai Meetei, Thoudam Doren Singh, and Sivaji Bandyopadhyay. 2019. Wat2019: English-hindi translation on hindi visual genome dataset. In *Proceedings of the 6th Workshop on Asian Translation*, pages 181–188.

Kishore Papineni, Salim Roukos, Todd Ward, and Wei-Jing Zhu. 2002. Bleu: a method for automatic evaluation of machine translation. In *Proceedings of the 40th Annual Meeting of the Association for Computational Linguistics*, pages 311–318, Philadelphia, Pennsylvania, USA. Association for Computational Linguistics.

Shantipriya Parida, Ondřej Bojar, and Satya Ranjan Dash. 2019. Hindi visual genome: A dataset for multimodal english-to-hindi machine translation. *arXiv preprint arXiv:1907.08948*.

Bryan A Plummer, Liwei Wang, Chris M Cervantes, Juan C Caicedo, Julia Hockenmaier, and Svetlana Lazebnik. 2015. Flickr30k entities: Collecting region-to-phrase correspondences for richer image-to-sentence models. In *Proceedings of the IEEE international conference on computer vision*, pages 2641–2649.

Matt Post. 2018. A call for clarity in reporting BLEU scores. In *Proceedings of the Third Conference on Machine Translation: Research Papers*, pages 186–191, Brussels, Belgium. Association for Computational Linguistics.

Gowtham Ramesh, Sumanth Doddapaneni, Aravinth Bheemaraj, Mayank Jobanputra, Raghavan AK, Ajitesh Sharma, Sujit Sahoo, Harshita Diddee, Divyanshu Kakwani, Navneet Kumar, et al. 2021. Samanantar: The largest publicly available parallel corpora collection for 11 indic languages. *arXiv preprint arXiv:2104.05596*.

Devendra Sachan and Graham Neubig. 2018. Parameter sharing methods for multilingual self-attentional translation models. In *Proceedings of the Third Conference on Machine Translation: Research Papers*, pages 261–271, Brussels, Belgium. Association for Computational Linguistics.

Rico Sennrich, Barry Haddow, and Alexandra Birch. 2016. Neural machine translation of rare words with subword units. In *Proceedings of the 54th Annual Meeting of the Association for Computational Linguistics (Volume 1: Long Papers)*, pages 1715–1725, Berlin, Germany. Association for Computational Linguistics.

Alok Singh, Loitongbam Sanayai Meetei, Thoudam Doren Singh, and Sivaji Bandyopadhyay. 2021a. Generation and evaluation of hindi image captions of visual genome. In *Proceedings of the International Conference on Computing and Communication Systems*, pages 65–73, Singapore. Springer Singapore.

Alok Singh, Thoudam Doren Singh, and Sivaji Bandyopadhyay. 2021b. An encoder-decoder based framework for hindi image caption generation. *Multimedia Tools and Applications*.

Salam Michael Singh and Thoudam Doren Singh. 2020. Unsupervised neural machine translation for English and Manipuri. In *Proceedings of the 3rd Workshop on Technologies for MT of Low Resource Languages*, pages 69–78, Suzhou, China. Association for Computational Linguistics.

Ilya Sutskever, Oriol Vinyals, and Quoc V Le. 2014. Sequence to sequence learning with neural networks. In *Advances in Neural Information Processing Systems*, volume 27. Curran Associates, Inc.

Christoph Tillmann and Hermann Ney. 2003. Word Reordering and a Dynamic Programming Beam Search Algorithm for Statistical Machine Translation. *Computational Linguistics*, 29(1):97–133.

Ashish Vaswani, Noam Shazeer, Niki Parmar, Jakob Uszkoreit, Llion Jones, Aidan N Gomez, Ł ukasz Kaiser, and Illia Polosukhin. 2017. Attention is all you need. In *Advances in Neural Information Processing Systems*, volume 30. Curran Associates, Inc.

Shaowei Yao and Xiaojun Wan. 2020. Multimodal transformer for multimodal machine translation. In *Proceedings of the 58th Annual Meeting of the Association for Computational Linguistics*, pages 4346–4350, Online. Association for Computational Linguistics.

Zhong Zhou, Matthias Sperber, and Alexander Waibel. 2019. Paraphrases as foreign languages in multilingual neural machine translation. In *Proceedings of the 57th Annual Meeting of the Association for Computational Linguistics: Student Research Workshop*, pages 113–122, Florence, Italy. Association for Computational Linguistics.

Barret Zoph, Deniz Yuret, Jonathan May, and Kevin Knight. 2016. Transfer learning for low-resource neural machine translation. In *Proceedings of the 2016 Conference on Empirical Methods in Natural Language Processing*, pages 1568–1575, Austin, Texas. Association for Computational Linguistics.

Malta National Language Technology Platform: A vision for enhancing Malta's official languages using Machine Translation

Keith Cortis
Malta Information
Technology Agency
Gattard House,
National Road,
Blata l-Bajda, Malta
keith.cortis@gov.mt

Judie Attard
Malta Information
Technology Agency
Gattard House,
National Road,
Blata l-Bajda, Malta
judie.attard@gov.mt

Donatienne Spiteri
Office of the State Advocate
Casa Scaglia,
16, Mikiel Anton Vassalli Street,
Valletta, Malta
donatienne.spiteri
@stateadvocate.mt

Abstract

In this paper we introduce a vision towards establishing the Malta National Language Technology Platform; an ongoing effort that aims to provide a basis for enhancing Malta's official languages, namely Maltese and English, using Machine Translation. This will contribute towards the current niche of Language Technology support for the Maltese low-resource language, across multiple computational linguistics fields, such as speech processing, machine translation, text analysis, and multimodal resources. The end goals are to remove language barriers, increase accessibility, foster cross-border services, and most importantly to facilitate the preservation of the Maltese language.

1 Introduction

Work in Computational Linguistics and Natural Language Processing (NLP) has been gaining a lot of traction in recent years. Particularly with the advance of the World Wide Web, this field now has access to thousands of languages. Whilst initially the field focused on a smaller number of these languages, namely high-resourced languages such as English, Chinese, and German, it is becoming increasingly evident that substantial effort needs to be invested in low-resource languages, particularly those at risk of becoming extinct. Here, the Web could act either as a catalyst to the disappearance of such languages, especially if the language is spoken by minorities, or it could help preserve such languages if the relevant resources, including NLP tools, are made available.

In the research conducted by Rosner and Joachimsen, the authors conclude that the level of technological support for Maltese, compared to that for other European languages, is extremely low, giving rise to the threat of "digital extinction" for the language (Rosner and Joachimsen, 2012). In this context, *"digital extinction"* refers to the possibility that Maltese, while possibly maintaining its status as a national tongue with institutional support and recognition, is nevertheless virtually absent from digital media.

The current state of language technology (LT) support for the Maltese language is weak or provides no support with respect to **speech processing**, **machine translation** (MT), **text analysis** and **speech and text resources**. Considering this current state of Maltese LT support, the English language has become the default language of choice across most technological devices in Malta, simply because there are more language resources and tools available and they are easier to use. Taking this in consideration, prominence should also be directed towards Maltese language resources and tools, such as lexicons, corpora, lexical resources, language models and natural language processing tools, that can be used by any Artificial Intelligence (AI) technology initiative.

Investment in language technologies, tools and resources, especially those focused on low-resourced languages such as Maltese, provides the opportunity to address the complex issue of multilingualism in Europe and thus caters for citizens' needs to communicate across the language borders of the European Common Market. The developed Maltese language tools and resources can also feed into the European Language Grid (Rehm et al., 2021); the primary cloud-based platform for LT in Europe. The aim of this platform is to boost the Multilingual Digital Single Market towards a prosperous European LT community, which shall create jobs, new markets and new opportunities.

In a concrete effort to increase resources in the Maltese language and facilitating the preservation of the Maltese language, this paper presents a vision towards the development of a National Language Technology Platform (NLTP) for Malta.

Proceedings of the First Workshop on Multimodal Machine Translation for Low Resource Languages (MMTLRL 2021), in conjuction with RANLP-2021, September 7, 2021. pages 12–19
https://doi.org/10.26615/978-954-452-073-1_003

This work is part of a CEF Telecom – Automated Translation (EU) project which has started in April 2021, whereby Latvia, Estonia, Croatia, Iceland, and Malta shall be developing a NLTP for each country for language tools and resources[1]. With respect to Malta, the Maltese adaptation of the NLTP will be implemented through a collaboration between the Malta Information Technology Agency (MITA); the technology partner responsible for Malta's NLTP development, the Office of the State Advocate (OSA); a pilot partner with a specific focus on the legal domain, and the University of Malta (UM); a research partner who shall be working on neural approaches towards multimodal machine translation (MMMT). Moreover, the Malta NLTP aligns with Malta's Strategy and Vision for Artificial Intelligence (Schembri, 2019) where the country is investing in the development of Maltese language tools and resources.

2 Multilingualism Challenges

Multilingualism is considered to be a cornerstone value within Europe, where the language diversity is embraced as a basis to good administration (García, 2002). This linguistic diversity however creates many challenges stemming from language insularity, and impacts a number of domains, including public administrations, public e-services, and the cohesion of the European Union Digital Single Market (DSM).

In Malta, both Maltese and English are official languages, with Maltese –a language of Semitic origin written in the Latin script– being the national language. Maltese, an official language of the European Union, is spoken by 97.25% of the population (around 500,000 people)[2]. The public administration may use any of these languages for official purposes. Therefore, more prominence and importance need be given to the digital aspect of Maltese. Given that Malta is highly multilingual, the following are the main language challenges being faced, especially when the Maltese language is used for communication purposes:

- In the past decade or so, the number of foreign nationals living and working in Malta has increased. Therefore, the public administration deals with foreign nationals on a daily basis. The national "Novel Coronavirus" web page[3] shows an example of the country's multilingualism needs and challenges, where all information about COVID-19 has been translated to English, whereas other general information has been translated in over 20 languages. The following are some statistics supporting the need for such translations: Top 10 EU Nationals employed between 2002-2018 (Jobsplus, 2019a) and Top 10 Third Country Nationals employed between 2002-2018 (Jobsplus, 2019b).
- National media has a challenge to reach all foreign nationals in Malta especially in the current COVID-19 pandemic, where the main Government communication (mostly press conferences) was generally in Maltese. Therefore, such language barriers (MaltaToday, 2020) should be tackled for inclusion of foreign nationals living in Malta.
- Not all citizen-facing Government websites are available in Maltese and English. An analysis of the eighteen Government Ministries' (Gov.mt, 2021) websites identified only five of them which cater for both Maltese and English, with the other thirteen being localised in English only.
- Each entity within the public administration carries out their own language translation needs either in-house or through outsourcing to third parties. Most of the requested translations are from Maltese to English and English to Maltese. However, certain Ministries also carry out translations between other languages, such as between English and French, Italian, and German (Berzins et al., 2019).
- When translations are carried out in-house, no Computer Aided Translation (CAT) tools are used, although commercial tools are sometimes used (Berzins et al., 2019).
- No Government policy is available for sharing or pooling of translations and the respective translation memories. This is due to the lack of knowledge on the benefits of data contribution, both at a local and EU level (e.g., for eTranslation[4]) (Berzins et al., 2019).
- Lack of awareness on the importance of language resources and tools (Berzins et al., 2019).

[1] `https://ec.europa.eu/inea/en/connecting-europe-facility/cef-telecom/2020-eu-ia-0082`

[2] `https://languageknowledge.eu/countries/malta`

[3] `covid19health.gov.mt`

[4] `https://ec.europa.eu/cefdigital/wiki/display/CEFDIGITAL/eTranslation`

- Rare re-use of translated data (Berzins et al., 2019) both within the same entity/sector, at a cross-entity/sectoral and/or national level.
- Development of national digital services that are bilingual (Maltese and English) or multilingual are hindered due to the LT gap that exists between high-resourced languages, such as English, and other low-resourced languages, such as Maltese.
- Although it is possible for public entities to access the eTranslation system provided, this requires a specific login with the European portal. This operation might hinder the uptake of such a service.
- Lack of a platform that acts as a one-stop-shop for Maltese language tools and resources for all potential stakeholders, such as public administration, small and medium-sized enterprises (SMEs), researchers, and citizens.

The above are all different language challenges that motivate us further towards building a NLTP for sharing of language resources and tools with citizens, businesses, and the public administration, in particular ones that can cater for and support both the languages of Malta and other languages of foreign nationals living in Malta.

3 National Language Technology Platform

3.1 National Language Technology Platform Overview

The aim of the NLTP is to aggregate state-of-the-art LT tools and solutions in a single entry point. The NLTP will be an AI-driven solution that provides stakeholders with access to mature, tightly-integrated LT services, enabling the efficient and effective multilingual access to information, online services, websites, documents, etc. Stakeholders can include public administrations, businesses, and the general public. The end goals are to remove language barriers, increase accessibility, and foster cross-border services. The latter goals in fact are also priorities for the European Union (EU) and Member States (MS), as made evident by their increasing investment in various programmes intended to advance LT. This promotes democracy and civil society, cross-country cooperation, trade, investment, and European integrity.

Whilst the benefits of language technologies, tools, and services are already apparent, the use of many solutions is unfortunately still limited, potentially due to low discoverability and the specific applicability of such solutions. Therefore, through the matching and integration of existing solutions, including solutions developed in the CEF Telecom - Automated Translation programme, as well as other European and national programmes, the NLTP will provide translation and speech processing services that are easily customised to the specific requirements of each EU MS. More specifically, the adaptation will be carried out around the eTranslation building block supplemented with customised Neural Machine Translation (NMT) systems and speech processing tools, accessible through a unified user interface. The latter high-quality tools will be tailored for particular key domains within the public administrations and the relevant specific language, terminology, and communication style. The following are some of the LT tools and modules that will be available through the NLTP:

- eTranslation Digital Service Infrastructure (DSI);
- custom MT systems for specific domains and languages;
- terminology management services;
- translation memory (TM) accumulation and management functionality;
- widget for website translation;
- CAT environment;
- data repository; and
- speech-to-text and text-to-speech services.

In particular, the data repository shall be used for collecting source data from the stakeholders for further use and processing by the NLTP tools and modules. Furthermore, apart from the above tools and modules, integrated speech technologies will give access to information to people with disabilities such as visual or hearing impairments. The NLTP will therefore be an indispensable platform that enables stakeholders to access the necessary LT tools, thus enabling public administrations to simplify and automate their interactions with their citizens, businesses to target new markets, and citizens to access information and communicate also across borders.

3.2 Maltese Adaptation for the National Language Technology Platform

Malta's NLTP shall act as a central repository for interested stakeholders, including public entities, SMEs, researchers, citizens, and foreign nationals living and working in the country. The NLTP will continuously support the curation of Maltese language tools and resources, thus ensuring the presence of Maltese in digital environments. Moreover, the NLTP shall be adapted to the country's specific requirements, with the following being the most relevant ones:

- **Assessment and aggregation of linguistic tools and resources**: The necessary language resources (parallel and monolingual corpora) shall be collected and processed for general domain and domain-specific areas (including legal, culture, social security, health, and taxation) for the Maltese-English-Maltese MT system development. These resources consist of significant amounts of tokens per language –approximately 6.5 million per language for the parallel datasets within the legal domain[5], and approximately 250 million tokens for the Korpus Malti (Gatt and Čéplö, 2013) Maltese monolingual dataset (containing genres such as the press, literature, laws, parliament debates, and Wikipedia) and 1,000,000 words for an English monolingual dataset.
- **Development of custom MT systems**: A set of Maltese-English-Maltese custom NMT systems shall be developed using the linguistic resources collected and processed as listed above. The plan is to train a general domain NMT system and domain-specific systems based on the type of parallel data collected, language-specific terminology, and communication style used.
- **Multimodal data sources**: Certain Government data collected for the development of NMT systems contains data in multiple modalities, such as text and images, therefore, requiring multimodal data processing. Some data source examples are the Maltese laws (primary and subsidiary legislation)[6], and the Government services and information (e.g., the Government Gazette and Press Releases) provided by the Department of Information[7]. In the case of the latter, for example, the machine readable version of specific Government Gazettes represent certain data (e.g., tabular) as images.
- **Deployment**: MITA's Hybrid Cloud Enabling Infrastructure[8] is the platform of choice for the digital services of the Government of Malta.
- **National policies and directives**: Any national requirements, in terms of directives, such as Web Accessibility Directive (FITA, 2018) in accordance with the European Standard EN301549v1.1.2 (ETSI, 2016), and policies, such as the Government of Malta ICT Website Policy (MITA, 2019), shall be adhered to.

MITA shall provide the necessary assistance to any Maltese entity (ministries, departments, agencies, etc.) within the public administration who shows interest in integrating certain NLTP modules for further use within their domain, such as websites or internal systems. The "Webpage translation widget" is one of the modules that shall be integrated within citizen-facing Government websites to ensure that they are available in both Maltese and English.

Based on the requirements above, the following are the **main goals** that will define the success of the Malta NLTP:

- Increasing of language tools and resources for the Maltese low-resourced language, in particular as required for MT;
- Building and validating custom NMT systems targeting multiple domains (through pilots);
- Providing MT support and development of custom MMMT systems;
- Integration of NLTP with multiple eGovernment services and public web services;
- Enabling and facilitating the addition of other languages through the use of English or Maltese as an intermediary language, in order to provide further translations as required by the Maltese context; and
- Increasing efficiency in the public administration and reducing the expenditure on manual translations through the provision of automated MT services.

3.3 Legal Domain Pilot

The legal domain will be taken as an initial pilot for Malta's NLTP. The particular Maltese context, where both Maltese and English are official languages, provides an interesting basis for this pilot due to the specific requirements of the domain. In

[5] Quoted figure based on Chapters of the Laws of Malta from `https://legislation.mt/`, such as the Criminal Code, Civil Code, and Companies Act

[6] `https://legislation.mt/`

[7] `https://doi.gov.mt/`

[8] `https://cloud.gov.mt/`

fact, as defined by the Maltese Constitution, Maltese laws need to be enacted in both languages, however in case of any discrepancies between the two languages, the Maltese law prevails[9].

The drafting and the translation of Maltese legislation generally take place at Ministerial level or at more granular levels, such as specialised authorities, government agencies, and other public entities. When the latter are not in a position to provide a translation, the Legislation Unit within the Office of the State Advocate will carry out the translation itself, as part of its final review process of legislation. Although the Maltese version of the laws prevails over the English version in case of conflict, the vast majority of laws are first drafted in English and then translated into Maltese. This places a lot of responsibility on the translator who is usually further pressured by tight deadlines. For this reason, it is imminent that drafters and/or lawyer-linguists within the Maltese public administration are provided with appropriate language tools that facilitate the translation process and ensure consistency of terms and terminology across ministries and a multitude of domains.

The Laws of Malta comprise language and legal data going back almost 200 years. The data is bilingual, readily available and provides an excellent start for Maltese-English/English-Maltese AI solutions, such as MT in the legal domain due to its vastness and variety of areas it covers. The implementation of this pilot will therefore enable the relevant stakeholders to more easily and efficiently translate drafted legislation, facilitating the legislation enactment process and aiding in the reduction of any discrepancies in the respective texts.

4 Related Work

As a low-resource language, language technologies for Maltese are still lacking when compared to other languages, although there have indeed been developments in the domain in recent years. MT technology, especially MMMT technology, is still very limited.

4.1 Current Initiatives: Maltese Language Tools and Resources

This section provides a discussion on current landscape with respect to Maltese language tools and resources. These cater for multiple NLP tasks, however are limited to the textual modality, therefore highlighting the need for more research and development focused on other modalities, such as images, videos and spoken language.

The Maltese Language Resource Server (MLRS) (Rosner et al., 2006) currently serves as a central repository for Maltese language resources and tools built by the UM, such as a *tokeniser*, a *part-of-speech* (POS) tagger and *corpora*, such as the Korpus Malti. Ġabra[10] is an open *lexicon* for Maltese which contains several different lexical resources into one common database (Camilleri, 2013).

Borg presented a comprehensive and systematic treatment of Maltese *morphology* using machine learning techniques (Claudia Borg, 2015). The research resulted in a morphological classification system for verbs, nouns and adjectives, which although not sufficiently accurate, it can act as a basis for a more complete morphological analyser with broader coverage (Borg and Gatt, 2014). Ravishankar et al. developed a morphological analyser of Maltese, generated from a combination of affixation and form-generation rules. Evaluated over two corpora, the system fared reasonably well. (Ravishankar et al., 2017).

Tiedemann and van der Plas conducted a number of experiments on *dependency parsing*, in order to evaluate the practicality of cross-lingual learning for Maltese, as a low-resource language (Tiedemann and van der Plas, 2017). Despite encouraging results with model and data transfer, the outcome of the experiments indicate that cross-lingual parsing still lags far behind fully supervised models. Moreover, a new project focused on the development of a Maltese *spelling* and *grammar checker* solution (spellchecker) and owned by the Ministry for the National Heritage the Arts and Local Government, is currently in its initial stages.

The Multilingual Anonymisation toolkit for Public Administrations (MAPA) project is developing a multilingual anonymisation kit based on *Named Entity Recognition and Classification* (NERC) that is applicable for all EU languages, including Maltese (Ajausks et al., 2020). In (Cortis and Davis, 2021), the authors published a dataset that can be used for developing *opinion mining* tools, such as for *sentiment analysis* and language technologies for the Maltese official languages. It consists of user-generated content in English (high-resourced), Maltese-English (code-switched) and Maltese (low-

[9] `https://legislation.mt/eli/const/eng`

[10] `https://mlrs.research.um.edu.mt/resources/gabra/`

resourced) and has been annotated for multiple opinion dimensions, namely *subjectivity*, *sentiment polarity*, *emotion*, *sarcasm*, and *irony*.

With respect to *speech recognition*, the MASRI ("Maltese Automatic Speech Recognition") project[11] is focused on developing the first Automatic Speech Recognition (ASR) technologies for the Maltese language. To this end, the MASRI-HEADSET (Hernandez Mena et al., 2020), is the first spoken Maltese corpus designed for ASR. Recently, a system for Maltese ASR –bilmalti.com[12]– was launched online with the aim of advancing the speech-to-text technologies. As for *speech synthesis*, a Maltese speech engine (UM, 2020) shall be developed as further development of the Maltese text-to-speech Engine (FITA, 2012).

4.2 Machine Translation for Maltese

Rosner and Bajada tackle an issue in Statistical Machine Translation (SMT) where good quality translation is not strictly word-to-word (Rosner and Bajada, 2007). The authors propose a phrase extraction algorithm and carry out a preliminary evaluation on a set of bilingual texts. The latter indicated that parameterisation of the algorithm would improve the results.

Azzopardi carried out a large-scale evaluation of translation technologies for Maltese translators, including electronic dictionaries, termbases, corpora, spell-checking software, translation memory software, terminology memory software, terminology management software, and machine translation (Brandon Sam Azzopardi, 2015). For the latter, Azzopardi evaluated Google and Bing (the top two MT systems for Maltese) in a number of fields.

Habash et al. present Arab-Acquis; a dataset for evaluating MT between 22 European languages and Arabic (Habash et al., 2017). In the resulting benchmarking results on the 22 languages, the direct translation from English to Maltese scored the highest BLEU (Papineni et al., 2002) score, whilst the translation from Maltese to English scored around the average. For pivoting translation, the score for Arabic-English-Maltese translation is slightly below average, whilst the Maltese-English-Arabic translation scored the highest.

Aharoni et al. perform a large number of experiments to train massively multilingual NMT, involving up to 103 distinct languages and 204 translation directions simultaneously (Aharoni et al., 2019). Based on their results, the authors report that massively multilingual many-to-many models are effective in low-resource settings, and outperform previous state-of-the-art. The Maltese language was one of 102 languages paired with English, used for these experiments.

5 Envisaged Benefits

The following are the main benefits of Malta's NLTP:

- Language resources and tools are enablers to key technologies at a multimodal level, in terms of text, visual (video and image), audio, and speech, and to automate certain processes;
- Provide the Government with the required language resources and tools to build bilingual/multilingual digital services and AI tools and technologies;
- Enable more people and businesses to collaborate on LT initiatives, especially in MMMT;
- Ability to integrate and/or use the language resources and tools within key software environments;
- Improved citizen service support at a cross-sectoral level;
- Reachability in terms of different public entities within the public administration; and
- Reduction on costs for translation services.

6 Conclusions and Future Work

Malta's NLTP shall act as a central repository for Maltese language tools and resources, primarily in the context of automated translation, and act as a one-stop-shop for its stakeholders. Moreover, it shall continuously support the curation of any Maltese language tools and resources for multiple domains, thus ensuring the presence of the currently low-resourced Maltese language in digital environments and countering the threat of *"digital extinction"* of the language. This project is anticipated to leave both a social and economic impact to the Maltese society and economy which benefits the citizens, the public administration, private entities, and academic institutions.

Acknowledgments

This work is funded by the European Commission under Connecting Europe Facility (CEF) - Telecommunications Sector (Agreement No. INEA/CEF/ICT/A2020/2278398).

[11]https://www.um.edu.mt/projects/masri/
[12]https://www.bilmalti.com/

References

Roee Aharoni, Melvin Johnson, and Orhan Firat. 2019. Massively multilingual neural machine translation. In *Proceedings of the 2019 Conference of the North American Chapter of the Association for Computational Linguistics: Human Language Technologies, Volume 1 (Long and Short Papers)*, pages 3874–3884, Minneapolis, Minnesota. Association for Computational Linguistics.

Eriks Ajausks, Victoria Arranz, Laurent Bié, Aleix Cerdà-i Cucó, Khalid Choukri, Montse Cuadros, Hans Degroote, Amando Estela, Thierry Etchegoyhen, Mercedes García-Martínez, et al. 2020. The multilingual anonymisation toolkit for public administrations (mapa) project. In *Annual Conference of the European Association for Machine Translation*, pages 471–472.

Aivars Berzins, Khalid Choukri, Maria Giagkou, Andrea Lösch, Helene Mazo, Stelios Piperidis, Mickaël Rigault, Eileen Schnur, Lilli Small, Josef van Genabith, Andrejs Vasiljevs, Andero Adamson, Dimitra Anastasiou, Natassa Avraamides-Haratsi, Núria Bel, Zoltán Bódi, António Branco, Gerhard Budin, Virginijus Dadurkevicius, Stijn de Smeytere, Hrístina Dobreva, Rickard Domeij, Jane Dunne, Kristine Eide, Claudia Foti, Maria Gavriilidou, Thibault Grouas, Normund Gruzitis, Jan Hajic, Barbara Heinisch, Verónique Hoste, Arne Jönsson, Fryni Kakoyianni-Doa, Sabine Kirchmeier, Svetla Koeva, Lucia Konturová, Jürgen Kotzian, Simon Krek, Gauti Kristmannsson, Kaisamari Kuhmonen, Krister Lindén, Teresa Lynn, Armands Magone, Hélène Mazo, Maite Melero, Laura Mihailescu, Simonetta Montemagni, Micheál Õ Conaire, Jan Odijk, Maciej Ogrodniczuk, Pavel Pecina, Jon Arild Olsen, Bolette Sandford Pedersen, David Perez, Andras Repar, Ayla Rigouts Terryn, Eirikur Rögnvaldsson, Mike Rosner, Nancy Routzouni, Claudia Soria, Alexandra Soska, Donatienne Spiteri, Marko Tadic, Carole Tiberius, Dan Tufis, Andrius Utka, Paolo Vale, Piet van den Berg, Tamás Váradi, Kadri Vare, Andreas Witt, Francois Yvon, Janis Ziedins, and Miroslav Zumrik. 2019. *Sustainable Language Data Sharing to Support Language Equality in Multilingual Europe - Why Language Data Matters: ELRC White Paper*, 2 edition. ELRC Consortium.

Claudia Borg and Albert Gatt. 2014. Crowd-sourcing evaluation of automatically acquired, morphologically related word groupings. In *Proceedings of the Ninth International Conference on Language Resources and Evaluation (LREC'14)*, pages 3325–3332, Reykjavik, Iceland. European Language Resources Association (ELRA).

Brandon Sam Azzopardi. 2015. *An evaluation of the computer-aided translation tools and resources available for Maltese translators*. Ph.D. thesis, University of Malta.

John J Camilleri. 2013. A computational grammar and lexicon for maltese. Master's thesis.

Claudia Borg. 2015. *Morphology in the Maltese language : a computational perspective*. Ph.D. thesis, University of Malta.

Keith Cortis and Brian Davis. 2021. A dataset of multidimensional and multilingual social opinions for malta's annual government budget. In *Proceedings of the International AAAI Conference on Web and Social Media*, volume 15, pages 971–981.

CCEN ETSI. 2016. Accessibility requirements suitable for public procurement of ict products and services in europe. `https://www.etsi.org/deliver/etsi_en/301500_301599/301549/01.01.02_60/en_301549v010102p.pdf`.

FITA. 2012. Erdf 114 maltese text to speech synthesis. `https://fitamalta.eu/projects/maltese-speech-engine-synthesis-erdf-114/`. ERDF 114 Maltese Text to Speech Synthesis.

FITA. 2018. Web accessibility directive. `https://fitamalta.eu/web-accessibility-directive-update/`. Web Accessibility Directive.

R Alonso García. 2002. The general provisions of the charter of fundamental rights of the european union. *European Law Journal*, 8(4):492–514.

Albert Gatt and Slavomír Čéplö. 2013. Digital corpora and other electronic resources for maltese. *Lancaster, UK*.

Gov.mt. 2021. Government of malta ministries and entities. `https://www.gov.mt/en/Government/Government%20of%20Malta/Ministries%20and%20Entities/Pages/default.aspx`.

Nizar Habash, Nasser Zalmout, Dima Taji, Hieu Hoang, and Maverick Alzate. 2017. A parallel corpus for evaluating machine translation between Arabic and European languages. In *Proceedings of the 15th Conference of the European Chapter of the Association for Computational Linguistics: Volume 2, Short Papers*, pages 235–241, Valencia, Spain. Association for Computational Linguistics.

Carlos Daniel Hernandez Mena, Albert Gatt, Andrea DeMarco, Claudia Borg, Lonneke van der Plas, Amanda Muscat, and Ian Padovani. 2020. MASRI-HEADSET: A Maltese corpus for speech recognition. In *Proceedings of the 12th Language Resources and Evaluation Conference*, pages 6381–6388, Marseille, France. European Language Resources Association.

Jobsplus. 2019a. Top 10 nationalities of employed eu nationals (2009-2019). `https://jobsplus.gov.mt/resources/publication-statistics-mt-mt-en-gb/labour-market-information/foreigners-data/#title2.1`. Top 10 Nationalities of Employed EU Nationals (2009-2019).

Jobsplus. 2019b. Top 10 nationalities of employed third country nationals (2009-2019). https://jobsplus.gov.mt/resources/publication-statistics-mt-mt-en-gb/labour-market-information/foreigners-data/#title3.1. Top 10 Nationalities of Employed Third Country Nationals (2009-2019).

MaltaToday. 2020. Employees cannot refuse to work if outlets have re-opened, minister says. https://www.maltatoday.com.mt/news/national/102136/watch_employees_cannot_refuse_to_work_if_outlets_have_reopened_minister_says/#.YPAJRugza72.

MITA. 2019. Gmict - website policy. https://mita.gov.mt/wp-content/uploads/2020/07/GMICT_P_0051_Website.pdf. GMICT - Website Policy.

Kishore Papineni, Salim Roukos, Todd Ward, and Wei-Jing Zhu. 2002. Bleu: a method for automatic evaluation of machine translation. In *Proceedings of the 40th annual meeting of the Association for Computational Linguistics*, pages 311–318.

Vinit Ravishankar, Francis M. Tyers, and Albert Gatt. 2017. A morphological analyser for maltese. *Procedia Computer Science*, 117:175–182. Arabic Computational Linguistics.

Georg Rehm, Stelios Piperidis, Kalina Bontcheva, Jan Hajic, Victoria Arranz, Andrejs Vasiļjevs, Gerhard Backfried, José Manuel Gómez-Pérez, Ulrich Germann, Rémi Calizzano, et al. 2021. European language grid: A joint platform for the european language technology community. In *Proceedings of the 16th Conference of the European Chapter of the Association for Computational Linguistics: System Demonstrations*, pages 221–230.

Mike Rosner and Jo-Ann Bajada. 2007. Phrase extraction for machine translation.

Mike Rosner, Ray Fabri, Duncan Attard, and Albert Gatt. 2006. Mlrs: a resource server for the maltese language. https://mlrs.research.um.edu.mt/.

Mike Rosner and Jan Joachimsen. 2012. Il-Lingwa Maltija Fl-Era Diġitali – The Maltese Language in the digital age. *META-NET White Paper Series. Springer, Heidelberg etc. http://www. meta-net.eu/whitepapers/volumes/maltese*.

Silvio Schembri. 2019. Malta: The Ultimate AI Launchpad - A Strategy and Vision for Artificial Intelligence in Malta 2030. https://malta.ai/wp-content/uploads/2019/10/Malta_The_Ultimate_AI_Launchpad_vFinal.pdf. Parliamentary Secretariat for Financial Services, Digital Economy and Innovation, Office of the Prime Minister.

Jörg Tiedemann and Lonneke van der Plas. 2017. *Bootstrapping a Dependency Parser for Maltese - A Real-World Test Case*, number 32 in Tributes, pages 355–365. College publications, United Kingdom.

UM. 2020. Um to further develop speech engine for the visually-impaired. https://www.um.edu.mt/newspoint/news/features/2020/02/maltese-speech-engine.

Low Resource Multimodal Neural Machine Translation of English-Hindi in News Domain

Loitongbam Sanayai Meetei[1], **Thoudam Doren Singh**[1], and **Sivaji Bandyopadhyay**[1]

[1]Centre for Natural Language Processing (CNLP) & Dept. of CSE , NIT Silchar, India
{loisanayai,thoudam.doren,sivaji.cse.ju}@gmail.com

Abstract

Incorporating multiple input modalities in a machine translation (MT) system is gaining popularity among MT researchers. Unlike the publicly available dataset for Multimodal Machine Translation (MMT) tasks, where the captions are short image descriptions, the news captions provide a more detailed description of the contents of the images. As a result, numerous named entities relating to specific persons, locations, etc., are found. In this paper, we acquire two monolingual news datasets reported in English and Hindi paired with the images to generate a synthetic English-Hindi parallel corpus. The parallel corpus is used to train the English-Hindi Neural Machine Translation (NMT) and an English-Hindi MMT system by incorporating the image feature paired with the corresponding parallel corpus. We also conduct a systematic analysis to evaluate the English-Hindi MT systems with 1) more synthetic data and 2) by adding back-translated data. Our finding shows improvement in terms of BLEU scores for both the NMT (+8.05) and MMT (+11.03) systems.

1 Introduction

With the implementation of encoder-decoder architecture (Cho et al., 2014; Luong et al., 2015; Vaswani et al., 2017), MT systems have undergone quality enhancement. Instead of using text as the only input in an MT system, the current trend has also started exploring Multimodal Machine Translation (MMT), where multiple input modalities such as visual modality are incorporated along with the text as an input to the MT system. Using the MMT system has shown improvement in the translated text output as compared to the NMT system (Huang et al., 2016; Caglayan et al., 2016; Elliott and Kádár, 2017; Caglayan et al., 2019). To analyse the benefits of using multiple modalities of input, various shared tasks are organized (WAT2019 Multi-Modal Translation Task[1], WMT2018[2], VMT Challenge[3]). However, the image descriptions in the majority of current datasets are made up of user-captioned or created by crowdsourcing. On the other hand, the captions present in the news details the contents of the image with better clarity, and as a result, contain many named entities relating to specific individuals, locations, organizations, etc. For example, in Figure 1, the caption *"The old looking ship is sailing at sunset"* correctly depicts the image on some levels, yet it fails to portray the picture's higher-level scenario as described in the caption on the left.

Figure 1: Examples from our dataset (left) and multi30k (right).

Limited data resources set back the development of a machine learning-based system. The lack of high-quality training parallel dataset poses a considerable challenge in developing an MT system for low resource languages. For an extremely low resource language pair, training with NMT, which is a data-driven approach, often reports to poor performance of the MT system (Singh and Hujon, 2020; Singh and Singh, 2020). As such, re-

[1]https://ufal.mff.cuni.cz/hindi-visual-genome/wat-2019-multimodal-task
[2]http://www.statmt.org/wmt18/multimodal-task.html
[3]https://eric-xw.github.io/vatex-website/translation_2020.html

Proceedings of the First Workshop on Multimodal Machine Translation for Low Resource Languages (MMTLRL 2021), in conjuction with RANLP-2021, September 7, 2021. pages 20–29
https://doi.org/10.26615/978-954-452-073-1_004

searchers have investigated various models to augment the dataset using the monolingual corpus, such as back-translation (Sennrich et al., 2015a), incorporating language model train on monolingual dataset (Gulcehre et al., 2015), etc. The approach reported in (Sennrich et al., 2015a; Calixto et al., 2017a) acquire an additional training dataset by back-translating from a monolingual target dataset. In this paper, we acquire monolingual news datasets reported in English and Hindi, which are used to generate a synthetic parallel corpus. English→Hindi NMT systems are trained by using the parallel corpus. We train English→Hindi MMT systems by incorporating the image as a feature paired with the corresponding parallel corpus. We also conduct a systematic analysis to evaluate the MT systems by training with 1) more synthetic data and 2) adding back-translated data. Belonging to the same language family, Indo-European, English, and Hindi follow different word orders: Subject Verb Object (SVO) and Subject Object Verb (SOV).

The remainder of this paper is organized as follows: Section 2 discuss the previous related works followed by the framework of our model in Section 3. Section 4 details our system set up and Section 5 illustrates the analysis of our result. Section 6 sums up the conclusion and future works.

2 Related Works

A review of the machine translation-related works is discussed in this section. Based on the encoder-decoder model of the NMT model, various architectures are built to improve the performance of MT systems (Sutskever et al., 2014; Bahdanau et al., 2014). For both the encoder and the decoder, Sutskever et al. (2014) stacked numerous layers of an RNN with a Long Short-Term Memory (LSTM) (Hochreiter and Schmidhuber, 1997) hidden unit. Bahdanau et al. (2014) introduced an attention mechanism where the decoder attends to various sections of the source text at each step of generation of the output. While the model enhances the translation of long sentences due to its sequential nature, each hidden state depends on the output of the previous hidden state resulting in a large consumption of computational power.

Gage (1994) introduced a method for data compression, BPE, which iteratively substitutes single, unused bytes for common bytes pairs in a sequence. Sennrich et al. (2015b) proposed a method for word segmentation to deal with an open vocabulary problem. Instead of common byte pairs, the method combines characters or character sequences. Provilkov et al. (2019) achieves a better MT system by introducing a dropout in BPE (Sennrich et al., 2015b), the BPE-dropout excludes some merges randomly, resulting in the same word with different segmentation.

Vinyals et al. (2015) introduced a neural and probabilistic framework to generate image captions. The model comprises a vision Convolution Neural Network (CNN), which is followed by a Recurrent Neural Network (RNN) to generate a language. Extracting global features from an image to incorporate into attention-based NMT, Calixto et al. (2017b) introduced various multimodal neural machine translation models. Using the features of an image to initialize the encoder hidden state is reported to be the best performing among other models. Using Hindi Visual Genome (Parida et al., 2019) dataset, Meetei et al. (2019) carried out an MMT for the English-Hindi language pair. The author reported that the use of multiple modalities as an input improves the MT system.

Various approaches to data augmentation are applied to mitigate the scarcity of parallel training datasets for MT tasks. Gulcehre et al. (2015) used a language model train on a monolingual dataset, achieving an improvement of up to 1.96 BLEU on Turkish-English, a low resource language pair. The author also reported that domain similarity between monolingual dataset and target task was the key factor to use an external language model to improve the MT system. Sennrich et al. (2015a) carried out the back-translation of monolingual target text into the source text, thereby generating an additional training dataset. The author reported that even the limited amount of back-translated in-domain monolingual datasets could be utilized efficiently for domain adaptation. Calixto et al. (2017a) used a text-only NMT model train on Multi30k (Elliott et al., 2016) dataset (German-English), without images to back-translate German descriptions in the Multi30k into English and included it as additional training data.

3 Methodology

In our experiment, news articles reported in English and Hindi along with the corresponding images in the articles are collected. After subjecting to a pre-processing step, the collected dataset is

	sentences	images
$en\text{-}hi_{st}$	80900	80900
$hi\text{-}en_{st}$	42400	42400

Table 1: Machine translated datasets, $en\text{-}hi_{st}$ and $hi\text{-}en_{st}$

machine translated to generate a synthetic parallel dataset. MT systems are trained with various settings by using the synthetic parallel dataset.

3.1 Building synthetic English-Hindi and Hindi-English dataset

News articles reported in English along with their corresponding images are collected from a national news channel, *India TV*[4], for the period June 2010 to May 2020. After filtering the articles where the image is absent, the collected dataset comprises 80900 and 42400 news articles reported in English and Hindi, respectively. The dataset is gathered by utilizing a web-scraper built in-house. In order to prepare the experimental dataset, we separate the headline from each of the news article items, which is considered as the description for the corresponding image. Apart from a standard single sentence, the image description comprises single or multiple phrases. Using IndicTrans[5] (Kakwani et al., 2020), which is an NMT system, we build two machine translated parallel datasets, namely English-Hindi ($en\text{-}hi_{st}$) and Hindi-English ($hi\text{-}en_{st}$), Table 1.

3.2 Machine Translation Systems

Our experiment used both NMT and MMT approaches to train English→Hindi MT systems in our parallel news dataset.

3.2.1 Neural Machine Translation (NMT)

For a source sentence x, the translation task tries to find a target sentence y that maximizes the conditional probability of y given x. We followed the attention model of Bahdanau et al. (2014) by using a bi-LSTM (Sutskever et al., 2014) in the encoder and an alignment model paired with an LSTM in the decoder model. The bi-LSTM generates a sequence of annotations (h_1, h_2,...,h_N) = h_i for each input sentence, x = ($x_1, x_2, ..., x_N$). $h_i = [\vec{h_i};\overleftarrow{h_i}]$ is the concatenation of forward hidden state, $\vec{h_i}$ and backward hidden state, $\overleftarrow{h_i}$ in the encoder at time step i. The attention mechanism focuses on specific input vectors in the input sequence based on the attention weights.

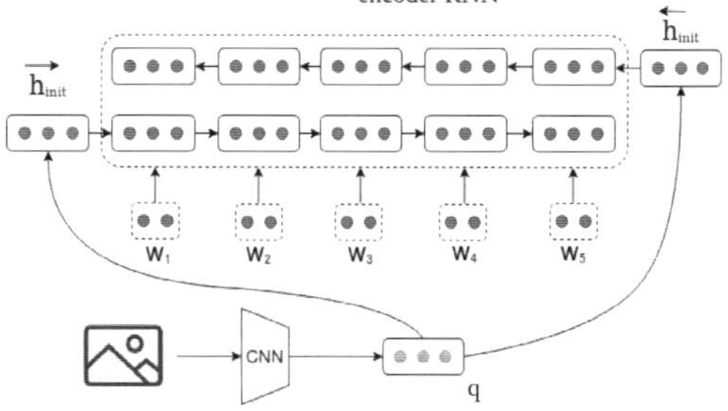

Figure 2: MMT model

3.2.2 Multimodal Machine Translation (MMT)

We train the MMT systems using the image from the news article paired with the English-Hindi parallel dataset. Following the multimodal neural machine translation (MNMT) model (Calixto et al., 2017b), a deep CNN-based model is utilized to extract global features from the image, Figure 2. Global image feature vector (q $\in \mathbb{R}^{4096}$) is used to compute a vector d as follows:

$$d = W_I^2 \cdot (W_I^1 \cdot q + b_I^1) + b_I^2 \quad (1)$$

where W = image transformation matrices and b = bias vector.

Instead of using $\vec{0}$ (Bahdanau et al., 2014) to initialize encoder hidden states, two new single-layer feed-forward networks are utilized to initialize the states as:

$$\vec{h}_{init} = \tanh(W_f d + b_f) \quad (2)$$

$$\overleftarrow{h}_{init} = \tanh(W_b d + b_b) \quad (3)$$

where W_f and W_b are the multi-modal projection matrices that project the image features d into the encoder forward and backward hidden states dimensionality, respectively, and b_f and b_b as bias vectors.

4 Experimental Design

4.1 Dataset

With limited availability of parallel corpus, it is often difficult to train a data driven NMT system. Using the generated synthetic parallel dataset, we

[4]https://www.indiatvnews.com/

[5]https://indicnlp.ai4bharat.org/indic-trans/

	Text-Image	types	unique types	Avg_{SL}
train (T_b)	45000	en:472496, hi:548172	en:52841, hi:33617	en:10, hi:12
train (T_{ad})	T_b + 30900	en:796074, hi:923313	en:70371, hi:43945	en:10, hi:12
train (T_{bt})	T_b + 30900	en:806767, hi:1005549	en:64057, hi:52992	en:10, hi:13
train (T_{all})	T_b + 61800	en:1130335, hi:1380674	en:79574, hi:61419	en:10, hi:12
dev	3000	en:31437, hi:36576	en:10673, hi:7871	en:10, hi:12
test (t_1)	2000	en21038:, hi:24415	en:8089, hi:6176	en:10, hi:12
test (t_2)	2000	en:17105, hi:20854	en:5439, hi:5874	en:8, hi:10

Table 2: Statistics of our dataset and data partitioning.
en: English, hi: Hindi, Avg_{SL}: average sentence length

carry out a systematic analysis to evaluate the MT system by training with four experimental data settings.

- T_b: By randomly selecting 45000 parallel dataset from en-hi_{st} as the baseline training dataset.
- T_{ad}: T_b + an additional dataset of randomly selected 30900 from the remaining en-hi_{st} dataset.
- T_{bt}: T_b + an additional back-translated dataset of 30900 which are randomly selected from 42400 sentences (hi-en_{st}).
- T_{all}: Combining the above three training datasets i.e. $T_b + T_{ad} + T_{bt}$.

We use two holdouts test datasets, t_1 and t_2 from en-hi_{st} and hi-en_{st} (back-translated) respectively. The development dataset, however, is used from en-hi_{st} only. A detailed statistics of our dataset is shown in Table 2 where en-hi_{st} is split into training, development, and test datasets, whereas hi-en_{st} is used for training and test datasets.

Normalization and tokenization of English sentences are carried by using Koehn et al. (2007) and for Hindi sentences, we use *Indic NLP*[6]. By employing BPE-dropout (Provilkov et al., 2019), words in the pre-processed parallel corpus are segment into subword units for word embedding presentation before training the MT systems. A full regularization is applied with a dropout of 0.1 to the training dataset. Following the system design described in SubSection 3.2, we train our NMT and MMT systems using the processed dataset.

[6]https://anoopkunchukuttan.github.io/indic_nlp_library/

4.2 MT systems

Based on the four settings of training dataset, we train the following eight MT systems:

- NMT(T_b) and MMT(T_b): NMT and MMT systems trained with T_b respectively, *baseline models*.
- NMT(T_{ad}) and MMT(T_{ad}) : NMT and MMT systems trained with T_{ad} respectively.
- NMT(T_{bt}) and MMT(T_{bt}): NMT and MMT systems trained with T_{bt} respectively.
- NMT(T_{all}) and MMT(T_{all}): NMT and MMT systems trained with T_{all} respectively.

4.3 NMT system settings

The size of our encoder and decoder LSTM hidden states is set to 512. We use a batch size of 128 and a word embedding size of 512D for both source and target. The normalization method of the gradient is set to tokens. Along with other parameters such as learning rate at 0.01, Adam optimizer (Kingma and Ba, 2014), a dropout rate of 0.1, we train the system using early stopping, where training is stopped if a model does not progress on the validation set for more than 10 epochs.

4.4 MMT system settings

A CNN-based pre-trained model, VGG19 (Simonyan and Zisserman, 2014), is used to extract the global features of an image. By incorporating the features from the image and the processed text, we train our MMT systems with stochastic gradient descent and a batch size of 128. Early stopping is applied to stop the training when the MT system does not improve for 10 epochs on the development set. We carry out the implementation of our MT systems by using an NMT open-source tool

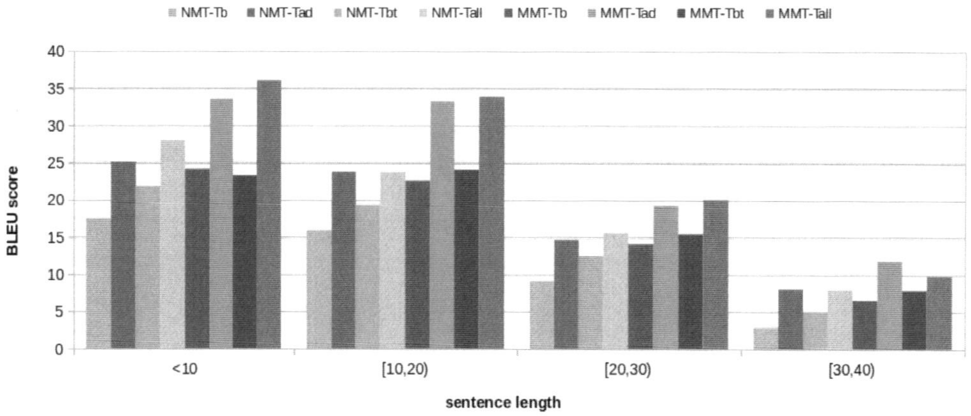

Figure 3: Evaluation on test dataset t_1

	BLEU		
	train	t_1	t_2
NMT	T_b	15.56	8.96
	T_{ad}	23.26(↑7.7)	13.47(↑4.51)
	T_{bt}	19.23(↑3.67)	11.70(↑2.74)
	T_{all}	23.61(↑8.05)	13.75(↑4.79)
MMT	T_b	22.20	14.54
	T_{ad}	32.30(↑10.1)	17.13(↑2.59)
	T_{bt}	23.43(↑1.23)	17.12(↑2.58)
	T_{all}	**33.23**(↑11.03)	**18.81**(↑4.27)

Table 3: Evaluation of NMT and MMT systems in terms of BLEU score.

based on OpenNMT (Klein et al., 2017). Subword-nmt[7] is used for encoding-decoding of the text dataset to and from subword units.

5 Results and Analysis

5.1 Based on Evaluation Metric

The automatic evaluation of our MT systems is reported using BLEU (Papineni et al., 2002). Table 3 shows a detailed evaluation of our MT systems on two test datasets, t_1 and t_2.

- **NMT systems:** NMT(T_{all}) outperforms the remaining NMT systems in both the test datasets, t_1 and t_2.
- **MMT systems:** MMT(T_{all}) outperforms the MMT systems in both the test datasets.
- **NMT vs MMT System:** The best MMT system, MMT(T_{all}) outperforms the best NMT system, NMT(T_{all}) by up to 9.62 BLEU score in t_1 and up to 5.34 BLEU score in t_2.

Training with additional datasets shows improvements in terms of BLEU scores for both the NMT and MMT systems. Although improvements are observed with the MT systems trained with the data augmentation approach, the BLEU score increases only by 1.23 while training with the additional back-translated dataset, T_{bt} for the MMT system. This shows that using an additional back-translated dataset improves our MMT system only by a small margin. It is observed that the performance of NMT(T_{ad}) and NMT(T_{all}) are almost comparable in terms of BLEU score, which indicates the poor effectiveness of T_{bt} in our experimental settings. Whereas, in the MMT system, MMT(T_{all}) outperforms the other MMT systems in terms of BLEU score by a reasonable margin. This indicates that incorporating image features in the MT system negates the bias introduced by the synthetic dataset to some extent. Furthermore, a large gap in terms of BLEU score is observed between t_1 and t_2. A likely cause is using more training dataset from $en\text{-}hi_{st}$ and the development dataset from $en\text{-}hi_{st}$ only.

Bucket Analysis: Figure 3 and Figure 4 shows bucket analysis where salient statistics are computed by assigning sentences over the bucket. After computing the BLEU score based on the length of the reference sentence, the analysis displays how well a system performs with shorter and longer sentences.

- t_1: Sentences in t_1 dataset are grouped into four buckets as shown in Figure 3. MMT(T_{all}) outperforms all the other MT systems by a large margin in most of the cases i.e. sentences with length less than 30. Although

[7]https://github.com/rsennrich/subword-nmt

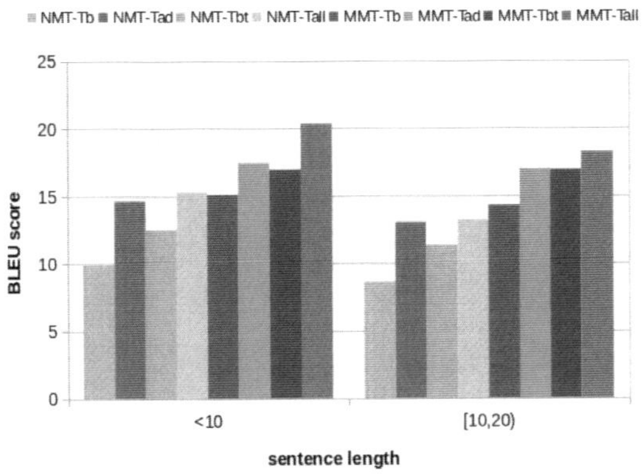

Figure 4: Evaluation on test dataset t_2

Score	Level Interpretation
0	No information is retained
1	Small amount of information is retained
2	Moderately retained information
3	Most of the information is retained
4	All information is retained

Table 4: Scale for Adequacy score.

the overall BLEU score of MMT(T_{bt}) is better than MMT(T_b), MMT(T_b) is observed to perform better than MMT(T_{bt}) when the sentence length is less than 10.

- t_2: As the maximum length of a sentence in the t_2 dataset is not more than 20, t_2 is grouped into two buckets, Figure 4. MMT(T_{all}) outperforms the other MT systems by a large margin irrespective of the sentence length. MMT(T_{ad}) is almost comparable with MMT(T_{bt}) in sentences with length [10-20).

Overall, the MT systems performs better when the length of a sentence is up to 10, and the performance declines as the length of a sentence increase above 10.

5.2 Adequacy and Fluency Analysis

Using adequacy and fluency indicators, we carried out human evaluations on our machine translated outputs. Adequacy indicates information retained in the generated translations, whereas fluency analyses generated translations primarily on grammatical rules. In our experiment, both adequacy and fluency are computed in the range of 0 to 4 scores. The meanings of the various score are summarized

Score	Level Interpretation
0	Incomprehensible
1	Disfluent
2	Non-native
3	Acceptable in terms of grammatical rules
4	Flawless and correct in terms of grammatical rules

Table 5: Scale for Fluency score.

	train	Adequacy	Fluency
NMT	T_b	1	1.5
	T_{ad}	1.55	2.1
	T_{bt}	1.35	1.85
	T_{all}	1.4	1.77
MMT	T_b	1.4	1.92
	T_{ad}	**1.95**	**2.35**
	T_{bt}	1.68	1.87
	T_{all}	1.8	2.1

Table 6: Evaluation of NMT and MMT systems in terms of Adequacy and Fluency score.

in Table 4 and Table 5. We use a sample output of randomly selected 100 sentences from each MT system to evaluate adequacy and fluency scores. The average score of the individual MT system is considered as our final score.

Table 6 shows the adequacy and fluency scores reported by our human evaluators. Comparison among the different NMT systems indicates no correlation between the manual evaluation and BLEU score. In the NMT system, adding a back-translated dataset in the T_{all} setting shows a negative effect in the fluency score, with NMT(T_{all}) scoring less than the NMT(T_{bt}). Similar observation is also observe among the different MMT systems. The adequacy and fluency score of MMT(T_{ad}) shows better results than MMT(T_{all}) by a small margin. When comparing between the NMT and MMT systems, correlation is found between the manual evaluation and BLEU score. Overall, in terms of adequacy and fluency score, the MMT system is more robust than the NMT system.

5.3 Translation Analysis

Table 7 and Table 8 shows a qualitative analysis on two examples from the test dataset (t_1) for the NMT and MMT systems. The words in "blue" highlights incorrect word(s) or gram-

	Input
Src:	Pune: One nurse tests COVID-19 positive, 30 others quarantined
Ref:	पुणे में एक नर्स कोविड–१९ पॉजिटिव, ३० अन्य पृथक–वास में (pune mein ek nurse covid-19 positive, 30 anay prthak-vaas mein)

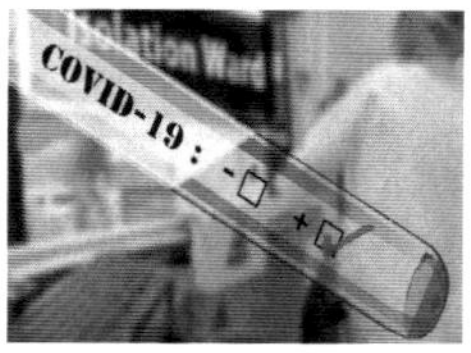

	NMT Model Outputs
T_b	पुणे में एक महीने का कोविड–१९ पॉजिटिव पॉजिटिव आया, ३० अन्य लोगों को क्वारंटीन किया गया (pune mein ek maheene ka covid-19 positive positive anya, 30 anya logon ko quarantine kiya gaya) "One month of Covid-19 positive positive others came in Pune, 30 others were quarantined"
T_{ad}	पुणे में एक व्यक्ति कोविड–१९ से संक्रमित, ३० अन्य लोगों को क्वारंटीन किया गया (pune mein ek vyakti covid-19 se sankramit, 30 anya logon ko quarantine kiya gaya) "One person infected with Covid-19 in Pune, 30 others have been quarantined"
T_{bt}	पुणे में एक कोविड–१९ से संक्रमित पाए गए कोविड–१९ से संक्रमित (pune mein ek covid-19 se sankramit pae gae covid-19 se sankramit) "One found infected with Covid-19 in Pune infected with Covid-19"
T_{all}	पुणे में एक नर्स कोविड–१९ पॉजिटिव पाए गए (pune mein ek nurse covid-19 positive pae gae) "One nurse in Pune found to be Covid-19 positive"
	MMT Model Outputs
T_b	पुणे में एक नर्स कोविड–१९ से संक्रमित, ३० अन्य संक्रमित (pune mein ek nurse Covid-19 se sankramit, 30 anya sankramit) "One nurse infected with Covid-19 in Pune, 30 others infected"
T_{ad}	पुणे: एक नर्स का कोविड–१९ टेस्ट पॉजिटिव आया, ३० अन्य लोग क्वारंटीन (pune: ek nurse ka Covid-19 test positive aaya, 30 anya log quarantine) "Pune: One nurse tested positive for COVID-19, 30 others in quarantine"
T_{bt}	पुणे में एक नर्स कोविड–१९ से संक्रमित, ३० अन्य को क्वारंटीन किया गया (pune mein ek nurse covid-19 se sankramit, 30 anya ko quarantine kiya gaya) "One nurse infected with Covid-19 in Pune, 30 others were quarantined"
T_{all}	पुणे में नर्स का कोविड–१९ टेस्ट पॉजिटिव आया, ३० अन्य को क्वारंटीन किया गया (pune mein nurse ka covid-19 test positive aya, 30 anya ko quarantine kiya gaya) "Covid-19 test of a nurse came out positive in Pune, 30 others were quarantined"

Table 7: Input Output sample 1

matically error in the translation output whereas, words in "magenta" highlights incorrectly translated word(s). NMT(T_b) and NMT(T_{bt}) generate translations with low fluency, where part of the sentence is grammatically incorrect, which in turn affects the adequacy of the translated text. Though the MMT(T_b) and MMT(T_{bt}) generates a translation with good fluency, the model fails to convey the words like *"quarantined"*, *"landslide"* and instead translates as *"quarantined"*→ "infected" , *"landslide"*→ "disturbance", and *"landslide"*→ "collision" thereby reducing the adequacy of the translated text. As reported in the adequacy and fluency evaluation in Table 6, T_{all} performs poorly in the NMT system with the translation output missing part of the source sentence as shown in the sample examples. MMT(T_{ad}) and NMT(T_{all}) generate translations that are grammatically correct and convey correct meaning as the input sentence.

6 Conclusion and Future Work

The lack of a high-quality parallel dataset for the MT tasks is one of the major challenges, especially for low resource languages. In this work, we collected two monolingual news datasets re-

	Input
Src:	After major landslide on Mumbai-Pune Expressway, Railways announces special 
Ref:	मुंबई–पुणे एक्सप्रेसवे पर भूस्खलन के बाद रेलवे ने विशेष ट्रेनों की घोषणा की (mumbai-pune expressway par bhooskhalan ke baad railway ne vishesh trenon kee ghoshana kee)
	NMT Model Outputs
T_b	पुणे–पुणे एक्सप्रेसवे पर भगदड़, रेलवे ने स्पेशल स्पेशल ट्रेनें रद्द की (pune-pune expressway par bhagadad, railway ne special special trainon radd kee) "Stampede on Pune-Pune Expressway, Railways canceled special special trains"
T_{ad}	मुंबई–पुणे एक्सप्रेसवे पर भूस्खलन के बाद रेलवे ने विशेष ट्रेनों की घोषणा की (mumbai-pune expressway par bhooskhalan ke baad railway ne vishesh trainon kee ghoshana kee) "Railways announce special trains after landslide on Mumbai-Pune Expressway"
T_{bt}	पुणे–वे पर भूस्खलन के बाद रेलवे ने जारी की स्पेशल ट्रेनें (pune-ve par bhooskhalan ke baad railway ne jaaree kee special trainon) "Railways issued special trains after landslide on Pune-way"
T_{all}	मुंबई–पुणे एक्सप्रेसवे पर भूस्खलन के बाद भूस्खलन के बाद रेलवे की विशेष ट्रेनें (mumbai-pune expressway par bhooskhalan ke baad bhooskhalan ke baad railway kee vishesh trainon) "Railway special trains after landslide on Mumbai-Pune Expressway"
	MMT Model Outputs
T_b	एक्सप्रेसवे पर बड़ी गड़बड़ी के बाद रेलवे ने विशेष ट्रेनों की घोषणा की (expressway par badee gadabadee ke baad railway ne vishesh trainon kee ghoshana kee) "Railway announces special trains after major disturbance on Expressway"
T_{ad}	मुंबई–पुणे एक्सप्रेसवे पर भूस्खलन, रेलवे ने स्पेशल ट्रेनों की घोषणा की (mumbai-pune expressway par bhooskhalan, railway ne special trainon kee ghoshana kee) "Landslide on Mumbai-Pune Expressway, Railways announces special trains"
T_{bt}	रेलवे एक्सप्रेस एक्सप्रेसवे पर बड़ा टक्कर, रेलवे ने स्पेशल ट्रेनों की घोषणा की (railway express expressway par bada takkar, railway ne special trainon kee ghoshana kee) "Major collision on Railway Express Expressway, Railways announced special trains"
T_{all}	मुंबई–पुणे एक्सप्रेसवे पर बड़ा भूस्खलन, रेलवे ने की विशेष ट्रेनों की घोषणा (mumbai-pune expressway par bada bhooskhalan, railway ne kee vishesh trainon kee ghoshana) "Major landslide on Mumbai-Pune Expressway, Railways announces special trains"

Table 8: Input Output sample 2

ported in English and Hindi paired with the images to create a synthetic English-Hindi parallel corpus. A systematic analysis of English→Hindi NMT and English→Hindi MMT systems with various experimental datasets set up is conducted. An analysis of the dataset augmentation with the lack of a parallel dataset is carried out. We observe an improvement in the MT systems in BLEU scores for both the NMT and MMT systems with the data augmentation approach. Our results also show that when the training dataset is comprised of a synthetic dataset from both English→Hindi and Hindi→English directions, the back-translated dataset in T_{all} setting is more effective in the MMT system as compared to the NMT system. In the future, we would like to incorporate multiple modalities to improve the MT system.

Acknowledgments

This work is supported by Scheme for Promotion of Academic and Research Collaboration (SPARC) Project Code: P995 of No: SPARC/2018-2019/119/SL(IN) under Ministry of Education (erstwhile MHRD), Govt. of India. The authors thank the anonymous reviewers for their careful reading and their many insightful comments. The authors also thank the volunteers for their help in human evaluation tasks.

References

Dzmitry Bahdanau, Kyunghyun Cho, and Yoshua Bengio. 2014. Neural machine translation by jointly learning to align and translate. *arXiv preprint arXiv:1409.0473*.

Ozan Caglayan, Walid Aransa, Yaxing Wang, Marc Masana, Mercedes García-Martínez, Fethi Bougares, Loïc Barrault, and Joost Van de Weijer. 2016. Does multimodality help human and machine for translation and image captioning? *arXiv preprint arXiv:1605.09186*.

Ozan Caglayan, Pranava Madhyastha, Lucia Specia, and Loïc Barrault. 2019. Probing the need for visual context in multimodal machine translation. *arXiv preprint arXiv:1903.08678*.

Iacer Calixto, Qun Liu, and Nick Campbell. 2017a. Doubly-attentive decoder for multi-modal neural machine translation. *arXiv preprint arXiv:1702.01287*.

Iacer Calixto, Qun Liu, and Nick Campbell. 2017b. Incorporating global visual features into attention-based neural machine translation. *arXiv preprint arXiv:1701.06521*.

Kyunghyun Cho, Bart Van Merriënboer, Caglar Gulcehre, Dzmitry Bahdanau, Fethi Bougares, Holger Schwenk, and Yoshua Bengio. 2014. Learning phrase representations using rnn encoder-decoder for statistical machine translation. In *arXiv preprint arXiv:1406.1078*.

Desmond Elliott, Stella Frank, Khalil Sima'an, and Lucia Specia. 2016. Multi30k: Multilingual english-german image descriptions. *arXiv preprint arXiv:1605.00459*.

Desmond Elliott and Ákos Kádár. 2017. Imagination improves multimodal translation. In *Proceedings of the Eighth International Joint Conference on Natural Language Processing (Volume 1: Long Papers)*, pages 130–141, Taipei, Taiwan. Asian Federation of Natural Language Processing.

Philip Gage. 1994. A new algorithm for data compression. *The C Users Journal*, 12(2):23–38.

Caglar Gulcehre, Orhan Firat, Kelvin Xu, Kyunghyun Cho, Loic Barrault, Huei-Chi Lin, Fethi Bougares, Holger Schwenk, and Yoshua Bengio. 2015. On using monolingual corpora in neural machine translation. *arXiv preprint arXiv:1503.03535*.

Sepp Hochreiter and Jürgen Schmidhuber. 1997. Long short-term memory. *Neural computation*, 9(8):1735–1780.

Po-Yao Huang, Frederick Liu, Sz-Rung Shiang, Jean Oh, and Chris Dyer. 2016. Attention-based multimodal neural machine translation. In *Proceedings of the First Conference on Machine Translation: Volume 2, Shared Task Papers*, pages 639–645.

Divyanshu Kakwani, Anoop Kunchukuttan, Satish Golla, Gokul N.C., Avik Bhattacharyya, Mitesh M. Khapra, and Pratyush Kumar. 2020. IndicNLPSuite: Monolingual Corpora, Evaluation Benchmarks and Pre-trained Multilingual Language Models for Indian Languages. In *Findings of EMNLP*.

Diederik P Kingma and Jimmy Ba. 2014. Adam: A method for stochastic optimization. *arXiv preprint arXiv:1412.6980*.

Guillaume Klein, Yoon Kim, Yuntian Deng, Jean Senellart, and Alexander M Rush. 2017. Opennmt: Open-source toolkit for neural machine translation. *arXiv preprint arXiv:1701.02810*.

Philipp Koehn, Hieu Hoang, Alexandra Birch, Chris Callison-Burch, Marcello Federico, Nicola Bertoldi, Brooke Cowan, Wade Shen, Christine Moran, Richard Zens, et al. 2007. Moses: Open source toolkit for statistical machine translation. In *Proceedings of the 45th annual meeting of the association for computational linguistics companion volume proceedings of the demo and poster sessions*, pages 177–180.

Minh-Thang Luong, Hieu Pham, and Christopher D Manning. 2015. Effective approaches to attention-based neural machine translation. *arXiv preprint arXiv:1508.04025*.

Loitongbam Sanayai Meetei, Thoudam Doren Singh, and Sivaji Bandyopadhyay. 2019. Wat2019: English-hindi translation on hindi visual genome dataset. In *Proceedings of the 6th Workshop on Asian Translation*, pages 181–188.

Kishore Papineni, Salim Roukos, Todd Ward, and Wei-Jing Zhu. 2002. Bleu: a method for automatic evaluation of machine translation. In *Proceedings of the 40th annual meeting on association for computational linguistics*, pages 311–318. Association for Computational Linguistics.

Shantipriya Parida, Ondřej Bojar, and Satya Ranjan Dash. 2019. Hindi visual genome: A dataset for multimodal english-to-hindi machine translation. *arXiv preprint arXiv:1907.08948*.

Ivan Provilkov, Dmitrii Emelianenko, and Elena Voita. 2019. Bpe-dropout: Simple and effective subword regularization. *arXiv preprint arXiv:1910.13267*.

Rico Sennrich, Barry Haddow, and Alexandra Birch. 2015a. Improving neural machine translation models with monolingual data. *arXiv preprint arXiv:1511.06709*.

Rico Sennrich, Barry Haddow, and Alexandra Birch. 2015b. Neural machine translation of rare words with subword units. *arXiv preprint arXiv:1508.07909*.

Karen Simonyan and Andrew Zisserman. 2014. Very deep convolutional networks for large-scale image recognition. *arXiv preprint arXiv:1409.1556*.

Salam Michael Singh and Thoudam Doren Singh. 2020. Unsupervised neural machine translation for english and manipuri. In *Proceedings of the 3rd Workshop on Technologies for MT of Low Resource Languages*, pages 69–78.

Thoudam Doren Singh and Aiusha Vellintihun Hujon. 2020. Low resource and domain specific english to khasi smt and nmt systems. In *2020 International Conference on Computational Performance Evaluation (ComPE)*, pages 733–737. IEEE.

Ilya Sutskever, Oriol Vinyals, and Quoc V Le. 2014. Sequence to sequence learning with neural networks. In *Advances in neural information processing systems*, pages 3104–3112.

Ashish Vaswani, Noam Shazeer, Niki Parmar, Jakob Uszkoreit, Llion Jones, Aidan N Gomez, Łukasz Kaiser, and Illia Polosukhin. 2017. Attention is all you need. In *Advances in neural information processing systems*, pages 5998–6008.

Oriol Vinyals, Alexander Toshev, Samy Bengio, and Dumitru Erhan. 2015. Show and tell: A neural image caption generator. In *Proceedings of the IEEE conference on computer vision and pattern recognition*, pages 3156–3164.

Keynote Talk II
Multimodal Simultaneous Machine Translation

Lucia Specia
Imperial College London, England

Abstract

Simultaneous machine translation (SiMT) aims to translate a continuous input text stream into another language with the lowest latency and highest quality possible. Therefore, translation has to start with an incomplete source text, which is read progressively, creating the need for anticipation. In this talk I will present work where we seek to understand whether the addition of visual information can compensate for the missing source context. We analyse the impact of different multimodal approaches and visual features on state-of-the-art SiMT frameworks, including fixed and dynamic policy approaches using reinforcement learning. Our results show that visual context is helpful and that visually-grounded models based on explicit object region information perform the best. Our qualitative analysis illustrates cases where only the multimodal systems are able to translate correctly from English into gender-marked languages, as well as deal with differences in word order, such as adjective-noun placement between English and French.

Proceedings of the First Workshop on Multimodal Machine Translation for Low Resource Languages (MMTLRL 2021),
in conjuction with RANLP-2021, September 7, 2021. page 30
https://doi.org/10.26615/978-954-452-073-1_005

Multimodal Neural Machine Translation System for English to Bengali

Shantipriya Parida*, Subhadarshi Panda†, Satya Prakash Biswal♣, Ketan Kotwal*, Arghyadeep Sen♠, Satya Ranjan Dash♠, Petr Motlicek*

*Idiap Research Institute, Martigny, Switzerland
{firstname.lastname}@idiap.ch
†Graduate Center, City University of New York, USA
spanda@gradcenter.cuny.edu
♣The University Of Chicago, Chicago, USA
sbiswal@chicagobooth.edu
♠KIIT University, Bhubaneswar, India
{2081012,sdashfca}@kiit.ac.in

Abstract

Multimodal Machine Translation (MMT) systems utilize additional information from other modalities beyond text to improve the quality of machine translation (MT). The additional modality is typically in the form of images. Despite proven advantages, it is indeed difficult to develop an MMT system for various languages primarily due to the lack of a suitable multimodal dataset. In this work, we develop an MMT for English→Bengali using a recently published *Bengali Visual Genome* (BVG) dataset that contains images with associated bilingual textual description. Through a comparative study of the developed MMT system *vis-a-vis* a Text-to-text translation, we demonstrate that the use of multimodal data not only improves the translation performance improvement in BLEU score of +1.3 on the development set, +3.9 on the evaluation test, and +0.9 on the challenge test set but also helps to resolve ambiguities in the pure text description. As per best of our knowledge, our English-Bengali MMT system is the first attempt in this direction, and thus, can act as a baseline for the subsequent research in MMT for low resource languages.

1 Introduction

Over the last decade, deep neural networks (DNN) achieved state-of-the-art results for many tasks including computer vision, natural language processing, and speech processing—which encouraged researchers to design a system that will get benefit from the fusion of multiple modalities (Caglayan et al., 2016).

English Text: A girl playing tennis.
Bengali Text: একটি মেয়ে টেনিস খেলছে

Figure 1: A sample from the BVG dataset: an image with a specific region marked and its description in English and Bengali.

Multimodal Translation refers to the extraction of information from more than one modality where it is assumed that alternative views would be used for input data (Sulubacak et al., 2020; Yao and Wan, 2020; Elliott, 2018). The tasks and applications in multimodal translation involve translation of image captions, translation of video content, translation of spoken language, and others. These applications exploit more than one modality such as translation from video content includes audio and visual modality, and translation of image captions includes visual modality and caption text. Although there are different opinions on the performance of machine translation using visual modality but under limited resources, visual input generates better translation (Caglayan et al., 2019). It is observed that multimodal translation systems do

Proceedings of the First Workshop on Multimodal Machine Translation for Low Resource Languages (MMTLRL 2021), in conjuction with RANLP-2021, September 7, 2021. pages 31–39
https://doi.org/10.26615/978-954-452-073-1_006

not leverage the visual signal to produce the correct translation in case of mistakes in the source language sentence (Chowdhury and Elliott, 2019).

When images are considered as an additional modality, the recent research can be divided into two major approaches based on their utilization of image features for the MMT: processing the global image features (Calixto and Liu, 2017), and processing the object tags derived from the images (Gupta et al., 2021). Cross-lingual visual pre-training which learns multimodal cross-lingual representations also found effective in MMT (Caglayan et al., 2021).

Bengali (also known as *Bangla*) is an Indo-Aryan language widely spoken in India and Bangladesh and considered as the 6-th most spoken language of the world with approximately 230 million speakers. Although English-to-Bengali text-only parallel corpora (Haddow and Kirefu, 2020; Ramesh et al., 2021) are available for building MT systems (Hasan et al., 2019, 2020; Parida et al., 2020); the multimodal dataset for Bengali did not exist. Thus, English-Bengali MMT systems have not been developed until now. Recently, the first English-Bengali multimodal dataset: Bengali Visual Genome (BVG) has been published (Sen et al., (in press) —which has facilitated research and development of corresponding multimodal as well as image captioning tasks.

The primary objective of this paper is to develop an MMT system for Bengali where the multimodal input is provided as an image and its description in English. We have used the BVG dataset to demonstrate our MMT system. The BVG consists of image descriptions (or captions) in the bilingual corpus for a specific rectangular region in the image as shown in Figure 1. The bounded box region information (X, Y, width, height) for each of the images is provided in the dataset. The MMT system uses both text and the associated image to build the model to translate into the target Bengali text. We extracted the object tags as image features. Then the object tags are appended to the original English sentence which is then translated using mBART (Liu et al., 2020), a multilingual sequence to sequence model trained on millions of unsupervised multilingual sentences. We also perform a comparative study between the English-Bengali Text-to-text translation system and the built MMT system.

2 Related Work

There is limited research conducted in the domain of multimodal machine translation for Indian languages. Other than Hindi, no MMT system is available in other Indian languages due to the unavailability of the multimodal dataset for translation.

The Flickr30k dataset with Hindi description is used for multimodal NMT task by Dutta Chowdhury et al. (2018). They attempted to conduct multimodal translation from Hindi to English and examined whether visual image features can improve translation performance. They used synthetic Hindi descriptions for the Flickr30k dataset and provided validation and test corpus of English translations of the Flickr30k dataset. Similarly, Madaan et al. (2020) considered the Flickr30k dataset and asked five different crowd workers to provide Hindi translation of an image from the dataset and generated English captions with evaluating the quality of the translation.

Laskar et al. (2020) used Hindi Visual Genome 1.1 dataset (Parida et al., 2019) and used OpenNMT-py to build text-only NMT and multimodal NMT. They had used pre-trained CNN with VGG19 for extracting local and global features from the images for the multimodal translation. The multimodal NMT performs better as compared to text-only NMT.

3 Description of the MMT System

In this section, we describe the multimodal translation system developed for English →Bengali using the multimodal data which consists of images accompanying text. Our model is adapted from ViTA (Gupta et al., 2021)[1] which uses mBART (Liu et al., 2020), a multilingual sequence-to-sequence denoising auto-encoder that has been pre-trained using the BART objective (Lewis et al., 2020). Gupta et al. (2021) built a English→Hindi

[1] https://github.com/kshitij98/vita

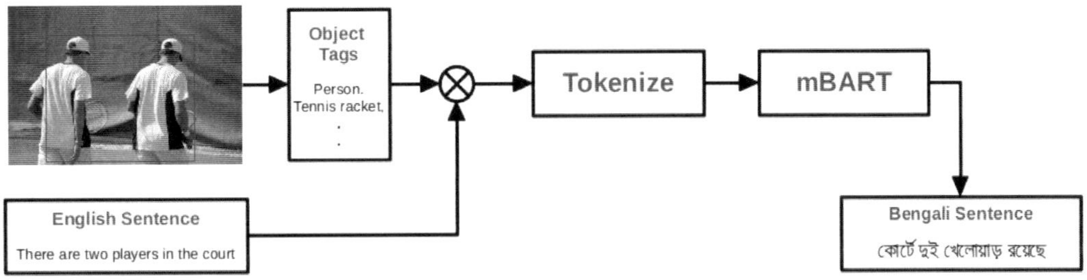

Figure 2: Multimodal machine translation. The object tags extracted from images along with the English source text input to the mBART to generate the Bengali translation output.

multimodal translation system by utilizing the object tags extracted from the images of the Hindi Visual Genome multimodal dataset (Parida et al., 2019) which is a dataset similar to the Bengali Visual Genome (see Section 4.1).

Similar to the ViTA approach, we first derive the list of object tags for a given image using the pretrained Faster R-CNN with ResNet-101-C4 backbone. Based on their confidence scores, we pick the top 10 object tags. In cases where less than 10 object tags are detected, we consider all the tags. The object tags are then concatenated to the English sentence which needs to be translated to Bengali. The concatenation is done using the special token '##' as the separator. The separator is followed by comma-separated object tags. Adding objects enables the model to utilize visual concepts which may not be readily available in the original sentence. The English sentences along with the object tags are fed to the encoder of the mBART model. The mBART's decoder generates the Bengali translations autoregressively. The block diagram of the multimodal translation using object tags is shown in Figure 2.

Gupta et al. (2021) applied ViTA for English to Hindi translation by using the mBART-25 model which has been pre-trained using the BART objective (Lewis et al., 2020). For this pre-training, only multilingual unsupervised data spanning 25 languages was used (Liu et al., 2020). Then they finetune the model for the machine translation task using 1.6 million English-Hindi parallel sentences. Finally, they finetune the model on the English-Hindi multimodal data with the addition of object tags by (a) first masking out 15% of the English tokens in the input and then (b) with no masking. For translating from English to Bengali, however, we do not perform a large-scale machine translation pre-training using a million training examples. We instead use the pre-trained mBART-50[2] model finetuned on the machine translation task in a one-to-many setup using multilingual data which contains merely 4487 English-Bengali parallel sentences (Tang et al., 2020). We take this pre-trained model and train it further on the machine translation task using the Bengali Visual Genome multimodal data by adding object tags to the English source sentences. Because of the scarcity of the pre-training machine translation English-Bengali parallel data (nearly 320 times smaller) as compared English-Hindi parallel data, our system represents a low-resource scenario.

Although the main approach we use is similar to the ViTA method by Gupta et al. (2021), we state the one modification in our implementation and the reason behind it. The original ViTA method stochastically masks out 15% of the tokens in the input English sentence. This is done to incentivize the model to utilize the object tags while generating the Bengali translation and not rely only on the English sentence. However, in our experiments, we do not mask out 15% of the English tokens. This is done because we already see gains above the text-only results without masking. Using masking can potentially improve the multimodal translation scores further.

[2]The mBART-50 model is trained using the same objective as the mBART-25 model. The difference is that the former supports 50 languages one of which is Bengali. Bengali is not supported by the latter.

4 Experiment Details

In this section, we first describe the dataset used followed by details of model training configurations.

4.1 BVG Dataset

Our experiments have been carried out using the BVG (Sen et al., (in press) dataset. The BVG dataset is segmented under four parts as the Training set, Development test set (D-Test), Evaluation test set (E-Test), and Challenge test set (C-Test). The BVG dataset statistics are shown in Table 1.

4.2 Translation using image and text modality

We used the large mBART one-to-many pre-trained model[3] in Huggingface Transformers library (Wolf et al., 2020). We did not freeze any model parameters during fine-tuning, therefore, the number of trainable parameters was 610M. The fine-tuning did not fit in the memory of a 28 GB GPU so we decreased the batch size to 1 and trained on a 48 GB GPU which was successful. The training time per epoch was 170 min. The model was fine-tuned for a maximum of 30 epochs. Adam optimizer (Kingma and Ba, 2014) was used with a learning rate of 1e-4. The training was stopped early if the development BLEU score did not improve for 5 consecutive epochs. The decoding beam size was set to 5. Model checkpoints were saved after every epoch and the best checkpoint was selected based on the development BLEU score.

4.3 Translation using text modality only

To demonstrate the impact of using image signals in the form of object tags, we conducted the experiments described in the previous section but without using any object tags. We did not modify any other configuration to ensure a fair comparison. We also note that adding object tags results in a large increase of tokens in each sentence. As a result, while not using object tags we observed that the training time per epoch reduced to 60 min, that is, the training was nearly 3 times faster.

[3]`https://huggingface.co/facebook/mbart-large-50-one-to-many-mmt`

4.4 Translation using Text-to-text transformer

In addition to the mBART pre-trained models, we also experimented with training a plain transformer model (Vaswani et al., 2017) from scratch. We first trained sentencepiece subword units (Kudo and Richardson, 2018) setting maximum vocabulary size to 8k. The vocabulary was learned jointly on the source and target sentences of the Bengali Visual Genome training dataset. The implementation was done using PyTorch (Paszke et al., 2019). The number of encoder and decoder layers was set to 3 each and the number of heads was set to 8. The hidden size was set to 128, along with the dropout value of 0.1. We initialized the model parameters using Xavier initialization (Glorot and Bengio, 2010) and used the Adam optimizer (Kingma and Ba, 2014) with a learning rate of $5e-4$ for optimizing model parameters. Gradient clipping was used to clip gradients greater than 1. The training was stopped when the development loss did not improve for 5 consecutive epochs. For generating translations, we used greedy decoding and generated tokens auto-regressively till the end-of-sentence token was generated or the maximum translation length was reached, which was set to 100.

5 Result and Discussion

We have used the popular machine translation metric BLEU (Papineni et al., 2002) for the automatic evaluation, computed using sacreBLEU toolkit (Post, 2018).

The development BLEU scores during training are shown in Figure 3.

The development BLEU score increases as the training progress. The mBART based scores (both Text-to-text and Multimodal) reach a notably high BLEU score even after one epoch of training. This is because of the prior knowledge acquired from pre-training, which is missing in the case of the Text-to-text transformer.

The MMT results on the D-Test, E-Test, and C-Test are shown in Table 2. The C-Test scores are consistently lower than D-Test and E-Test scores, indicating that the C-Test consists of more challenging segments which are harder to translate to Bengali. The Text-to-

Dataset	#Sentences	#Tokens	
		EN	BN
Train	28930	143156	113993
D-Test	998	4922	3936
E-Test	1595	7853	6408
C-Test	1400	8186	6657

Table 1: Statistics of BVG for experiments. The number of tokens for English (EN) and Bengali (BN) for each set are reported.

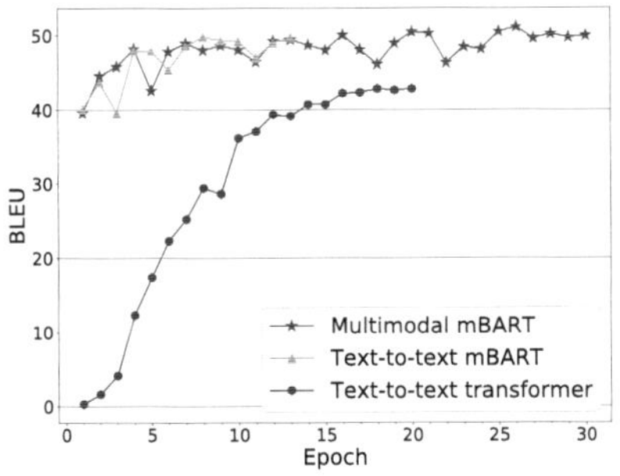

Figure 3: Development BLEU scores during training.

text mBART performs better as compared to the Text-to-text transformer model. The multimodal mBART performs the best overall.

The object tags added to the original English sentences provide more context about the image and enable the generation of a better translation, which is indicated by the higher overall BLEU scores. The improvement is seen in translating C-Test as well.

We performed the comparison of MMT system with the best Text-to-text translation system without using any image features. There is a performance improvement (BLEU score) of **+1.3** on D-Test, **+3.9** on E-Test, and **+0.9** on C-Test. Apart from performance, MMT systems help to resolve ambiguities as shown in the Table 3.

The MMT system can correctly translate the ambiguous word *court* which the Text-to-text MT system fails. We compared the translation output between both Text-to-text and MMT systems and observed the MMT system produces a better translation, correct word order, no ambiguity as compared with the Text-to-text MT system.

6 Manual Evaluation

To validate the automatic scoring, we manually annotated 100 randomly selected sentences from the C-Test set as translated by the Text-to-text machine translation system and MMT system. The annotation was performed by the native Bengali speaker. Bengali Captions in the MMT translation outcomes fall under five different sets where some of them are translated perfectly without any issue, some of them are very close to perfect, some of them have parts of speech or grammar issues, some of them have ambiguity in meanings, and some of them have lack of words than original annotation.

In this annotation, each annotated segment gets exactly one label from the following set (Parida and Bojar, 2018):

Flawless for translations without any error (typesetting issues with diacritic marks due to different tokenization are ignored),

Good for translations which are generally OK and complete but need a small correction,

Partly Correct for cases where a part of the segment is correct but some words are mistranslated,

Ambiguity for segments where the MT system "misunderstood" a word's meaning, and

Incomplete for segments that run well but stop too early, missing some content words. This category also includes the relatively rare cases where the Text-to-text or MMT system produced just a single word, unrelated to the source.

The manual evaluation results are summarized in following graph Figure 4. The MMT system generates more flawless and good translation output as compared to the Text-to-text system (see Figure 4). The Text-to-text system obtained more partial correct and incomplete translation output. It observed that still

MT System	D-Test BLEU	E-Test BLEU	C-Test BLEU
Text-to-text transformer	42.8	35.6	17.2
Text-to-text mBART	49.8	39.6	25.9
Multimodal mBART	**51.1**	**43.5**	**26.8**

Table 2: Text only and multimodal translation performance on the BVG dataset.

Input Image	**Input Caption**	**Text-to-text Result**	**MMT Result**
	The water bottle on the stand	স্ট্যান্ডে জলের বোতল	স্ট্যান্ডে জলের বোতল
		"Water bottle on the stand"	"Water bottle on the stand"
	Two people waiting to cross	দুজন লোক ক্রস অপেক্ষা করছে	দুজন লোক ক্রস অপেক্ষা করছে
		"Two people are waiting cross"	"Two people are waiting cross"
	Man standing on a tennis court	টেনিস কোর্টে দাঁড়িয়ে লোক	টেনিস কোর্টে দাঁড়িয়ে লোক
		"Man standing on a tennis court"	"Man standing on a tennis court"
	stamp on boy's left hand	ছেলেটির বাম হাতে স্ট্যাঙ্ক	ছেলেটির বাম হাতে স্ট্যাম্প
		"Stank on boy's left hand" (incorrect Bengali word 'Stank' obtained in T2T translation)	"Stamp on boy's left hand" (correct Bengali word 'stamp' obtained in MMT translation)
	fence around the court	আদালতের চারদিকে বেড়া	কোর্টের চারপাশে বেড়া
		"Fence around the court" (court is translated by T2T as *Judicial Court* in Bengali)	"Fence around the court" (court is translated by MMT as *Tennis Court* in Bengali)

Table 3: Samples of Text-to-text and Multimodal Translation obtained from the Text-to-text mBART and the Multimodal mBART systems. First two columns from left provide the input image and its corresponding English caption. The third and fourth columns are the Bengali captions generated by Text-only and Multimodal translation systems. For each Bengali caption, we also provide the English translation.

there are ambiguities exist in the translation output of both systems. Some translation samples are shown in Figure 5.

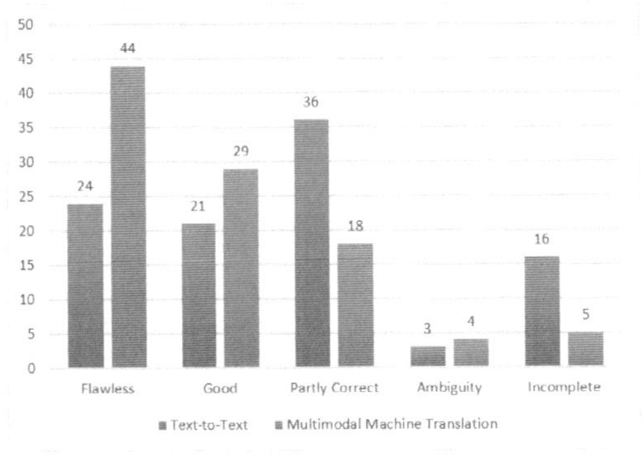

Figure 4: Manual evaluation summary. Out of 100 translation samples, five categories are chosen for observing Text-to-text and Multimodal Machine Translation Accuracy

7 Conclusion

In this paper, we build an English-Bengali MMT system utilizing bi-lingual text and the associated images which improves the translation quality (based on an automatic evaluation) and resolve ambiguities. Our work helps to build a better English-Bengali MT system and encourages researchers to explore the MMT system for Bengali. The future work includes exploring other state-of-the-art MMT systems on the BVG dataset and performs a comparison analysis (Tamura et al., 2020; Caglayan et al., 2021; Tan et al., 2020; Liu et al., 2021).

Acknowledgments

The authors Shantipriya Parida and Petr Motlicek were supported by the European Union's Horizon 2020 research and innovation program under grant agreement No. 833635 (project ROXANNE: Real-time network, text, and speaker analytics for combating organized crime, 2019-2022).

The authors do not see any significant ethical or privacy concerns that would prevent the processing of the data used in the study. The datasets do contain personal data, and these are processed in compliance with the GDPR and national law.

Flawless/Good:
Window on second level
দ্বিতীয় মেঝেতে উইন্ডোটি Gloss: Window on second level
Blue tennis court area
নীল টেনিস কোর্ট অঞ্চল Gloss: Blue tennis court area
Three baseball players on baseball field.
তিনটি বেসবল খেলোয়াড় মাঠে রয়েছে Gloss: Three baseball players on baseball field.
Partly Correct:
Railing on second floor of building
দ্বিতীয় তলায় রেলিংয়ে জেলিং Gloss: Gelling on second floor railing (output does not convey the intended meaning in the target language)
The hand is going to press a button
হাত জন একটি বোতামে যাচ্ছে Gloss: The hand is going to a button ('press' is completely omitted from the translated outcome)
Ambiguity:
Brown tennis court floor
আদালতে ধূসর রং Gloss: Brown color on Court Floor (Confusing Tennis Court with Judicial)
Street sign on a pole in English and Chinese
ইংলিশ এবং চীনা ভাষায় একটি মেরুতে রাস্তার চিহ্ন Gloss: Street sign on a pole in English and Chinese (confusing street-side pole with 'south pole and north pole' in Bengali)

Figure 5: Sample segment translations and their manual classification taken from MMT translation of Challenge Test Set.

References

Ozan Caglayan, Loïc Barrault, and Fethi Bougares. 2016. Multimodal attention for neural machine translation. *arXiv preprint arXiv:1609.03976*.

Ozan Caglayan, Menekse Kuyu, Mustafa Sercan Amac, Pranava Swaroop Madhyastha, Erkut Erdem, Aykut Erdem, and Lucia Specia. 2021. Cross-lingual visual pre-training for multimodal machine translation. In *Proceedings of the 16th Conference of the European Chapter of the Association for Computational Linguistics: Main Volume*, pages 1317–1324.

Ozan Caglayan, Pranava Swaroop Madhyastha, Lucia Specia, and Loïc Barrault. 2019. Probing the need for visual context in multimodal machine translation. In *Proceedings of the 2019 Conference of the North American Chapter of the Association for Computational Linguistics: Human Language Technologies, Volume 1 (Long and Short Papers)*, pages 4159–4170.

Iacer Calixto and Qun Liu. 2017. Incorporating global visual features into attention-based neural machine translation. In *EMNLP*.

Koel Dutta Chowdhury and Desmond Elliott. 2019. Understanding the effect of textual adversaries in multimodal machine translation. In *Proceedings of the Beyond Vision and LANguage: inTEgrating Real-world kNowledge (LANTERN)*, pages 35–40.

Koel Dutta Chowdhury, Mohammed Hasanuzzaman, and Qun Liu. 2018. Multimodal neural machine translation for low-resource language pairs using synthetic data. In *Proceedings of the Workshop on Deep Learning Approaches for Low-Resource NLP*, pages 33–42, Melbourne. Association for Computational Linguistics.

Desmond Elliott. 2018. Adversarial evaluation of multimodal machine translation. In *Proceedings of the 2018 Conference on Empirical Methods in Natural Language Processing*, pages 2974–2978.

Xavier Glorot and Yoshua Bengio. 2010. Understanding the difficulty of training deep feedforward neural networks. In *Proceedings of the Thirteenth International Conference on Artificial Intelligence and Statistics*, volume 9 of *Proceedings of Machine Learning Research*, pages 249–256, Chia Laguna Resort, Sardinia, Italy. PMLR.

Kshitij Gupta, Devansh Gautam, and Radhika Mamidi. 2021. Vita: Visual-linguistic translation by aligning object tags. *arXiv preprint arXiv:2106.00250*.

Barry Haddow and Faheem Kirefu. 2020. Pmindia– a collection of parallel corpora of languages of india. *arXiv preprint arXiv:2001.09907*.

Md Arid Hasan, Firoj Alam, Shammur Absar Chowdhury, and Naira Khan. 2019. Neural machine translation for the bangla-english language pair. In *2019 22nd International Conference on Computer and Information Technology (ICCIT)*, pages 1–6. IEEE.

Tahmid Hasan, Abhik Bhattacharjee, Kazi Samin, Masum Hasan, Madhusudan Basak, M Sohel Rahman, and Rifat Shahriyar. 2020. Not low-resource anymore: Aligner ensembling, batch filtering, and new datasets for bengali-english machine translation. In *Proceedings of the 2020 Conference on Empirical Methods in Natural Language Processing (EMNLP)*, pages 2612–2623.

Diederik P. Kingma and Jimmy Ba. 2014. Adam: A method for stochastic optimization. Cite arxiv:1412.6980Comment: Published as a conference paper at the 3rd International Conference for Learning Representations, San Diego, 2015.

Taku Kudo and John Richardson. 2018. SentencePiece: A simple and language independent subword tokenizer and detokenizer for neural text processing. In *Proceedings of the 2018 Conference on Empirical Methods in Natural Language Processing: System Demonstrations*, pages 66–71, Brussels, Belgium. Association for Computational Linguistics.

Sahinur Rahman Laskar, Abdullah Faiz Ur Rahman Khilji, Partha Pakray, and Sivaji Bandyopadhyay. 2020. Multimodal neural machine translation for english to hindi. In *Proceedings of the 7th Workshop on Asian Translation*, pages 109–113.

Mike Lewis, Yinhan Liu, Naman Goyal, Marjan Ghazvininejad, Abdelrahman Mohamed, Omer Levy, Veselin Stoyanov, and Luke Zettlemoyer. 2020. BART: Denoising sequence-to-sequence pre-training for natural language generation, translation, and comprehension. In *Proceedings of the 58th Annual Meeting of the Association for Computational Linguistics*, pages 7871–7880, Online. Association for Computational Linguistics.

Xiao Liu, Jing Zhao, Shiliang Sun, Huawen Liu, and Hao Yang. 2021. Variational multimodal machine translation with underlying semantic alignment. *Information Fusion*, 69:73–80.

Yinhan Liu, Jiatao Gu, Naman Goyal, Xian Li, Sergey Edunov, Marjan Ghazvininejad, Mike Lewis, and Luke Zettlemoyer. 2020. Multilingual denoising pre-training for neural machine translation. *Transactions of the Association for Computational Linguistics*, 8:726–742.

Aman Madaan, Shruti Rijhwani, Antonios Anastasopoulos, Yiming Yang, and Graham Neubig. 2020. Practical comparable data collection for low-resource languages via images. *arXiv preprint arXiv:2004.11954*.

Kishore Papineni, Salim Roukos, Todd Ward, and Wei-Jing Zhu. 2002. Bleu: a Method for Automatic Evaluation of Machine Translation. In *Proceedings of the 40th Annual Meeting of the Association for Computational Linguistics*, pages 311–318.

Shantipriya Parida and Ondřej Bojar. 2018. Translating short segments with nmt: A case study in english-to-hindi.

Shantipriya Parida, Ondřej Bojar, and Satya Ranjan Dash. 2019. Hindi visual genome: A dataset for multimodal english-to-hindi machine translation. *arXiv preprint arXiv:1907.08948.*

Shantipriya Parida, Petr Motlicek, Amulya Ratna Dash, Satya Ranjan Dash, Debasish Kumar Mallick, Satya Prakash Biswal, Priyanka Pattnaik, Biranchi Narayan Nayak, and Ondřej Bojar. 2020. Odianlp's participation in wat2020. In *Proceedings of the 7th Workshop on Asian Translation*, pages 103–108.

Adam Paszke, Sam Gross, Francisco Massa, Adam Lerer, James Bradbury, Gregory Chanan, Trevor Killeen, Zeming Lin, Natalia Gimelshein, Luca Antiga, Alban Desmaison, Andreas Kopf, Edward Yang, Zachary DeVito, Martin Raison, Alykhan Tejani, Sasank Chilamkurthy, Benoit Steiner, Lu Fang, Junjie Bai, and Soumith Chintala. 2019. Pytorch: An imperative style, high-performance deep learning library. In H. Wallach, H. Larochelle, A. Beygelzimer, F. d'Alché-Buc, E. Fox, and R. Garnett, editors, *Advances in Neural Information Processing Systems 32*, pages 8024–8035. Curran Associates, Inc.

Matt Post. 2018. A call for clarity in reporting BLEU scores. In *Proceedings of the Third Conference on Machine Translation: Research Papers*, pages 186–191, Belgium, Brussels. Association for Computational Linguistics.

Gowtham Ramesh, Sumanth Doddapaneni, Aravinth Bheemaraj, Mayank Jobanputra, Raghavan AK, Ajitesh Sharma, Sujit Sahoo, Harshita Diddee, Divyanshu Kakwani, Navneet Kumar, et al. 2021. Samanantar: The largest publicly available parallel corpora collection for 11 indic languages. *arXiv preprint arXiv:2104.05596.*

Arghyadeep Sen, Shantipriya Parida, Ketan Kotwal, Subhadarshi Panda, Ondřej Bojar, and Satya Ranjan Dash. (in press) 2021. Bengali visual genome: A multimodal datasetfor machine translation and image captioning. In *Proceedings of 9th International Conference on Frontiers of Intelligent Computing: Theory and Applications (FICTA)*. Springer.

Umut Sulubacak, Ozan Caglayan, Stig-Arne Grönroos, Aku Rouhe, Desmond Elliott, Lucia Specia, and Jörg Tiedemann. 2020. Multimodal machine translation through visuals and speech. *Machine Translation*, 34(2):97–147.

Hiroto Tamura, Tosho Hirasawa, Masahiro Kaneko, and Mamoru Komachi. 2020. Tmu japanese-english multimodal machine translation system for wat 2020. In *Proceedings of the 7th Workshop on Asian Translation*, pages 80–91.

Liang Tan, Lin Li, Yifeng Han, Dong Li, Kaixi Hu, Dong Zhou, and Peipei Wang. 2020. An empirical study on ensemble learning of multimodal machine translation. In *2020 IEEE Sixth International Conference on Multimedia Big Data (BigMM)*, pages 63–69. IEEE.

Yuqing Tang, Chau Tran, Xian Li, Peng-Jen Chen, Naman Goyal, Vishrav Chaudhary, Jiatao Gu, and Angela Fan. 2020. Multilingual translation with extensible multilingual pretraining and finetuning.

Ashish Vaswani, Noam Shazeer, Niki Parmar, Jakob Uszkoreit, Llion Jones, Aidan N Gomez, Ł ukasz Kaiser, and Illia Polosukhin. 2017. Attention is all you need. In *Advances in Neural Information Processing Systems*, volume 30. Curran Associates, Inc.

Thomas Wolf, Lysandre Debut, Victor Sanh, Julien Chaumond, Clement Delangue, Anthony Moi, Pierric Cistac, Tim Rault, Rémi Louf, Morgan Funtowicz, Joe Davison, Sam Shleifer, Patrick von Platen, Clara Ma, Yacine Jernite, Julien Plu, Canwen Xu, Teven Le Scao, Sylvain Gugger, Mariama Drame, Quentin Lhoest, and Alexander M. Rush. 2020. Transformers: State-of-the-art natural language processing. In *Proceedings of the 2020 Conference on Empirical Methods in Natural Language Processing: System Demonstrations*, pages 38–45, Online. Association for Computational Linguistics.

Shaowei Yao and Xiaojun Wan. 2020. Multimodal transformer for multimodal machine translation. In *Proceedings of the 58th Annual Meeting of the Association for Computational Linguistics*, pages 4346–4350.

Experiences of Adapting Multimodal Machine Translation Techniques for Hindi

Baban Gain
Indian Institute of Technology Patna
gainbaban@gmail.com

Dibyanayan Bandyopadhyay
Indian Institute of Technology Patna
dibyanayan@gmail.com

Asif Ekbal
Indian Institute of Technology Patna
asif@iitp.ac.in

Abstract

Multimodal Neural Machine Translation (MNMT) is an interesting task in natural language processing (NLP) where we use visual modalities along with a source sentence to aid the source to target translation process. Recently, there has been a lot of works in MNMT frameworks to boost the performance of standalone Machine Translation tasks. Most of the prior works in MNMT tried to perform translation between two widely known languages (e.g. English-to-German, English-to-French). In this paper, We explore the effectiveness of different state-of-the-art MNMT methods, which use various data oriented techniques including multimodal pre-training, for low resource languages. Although the existing methods works well on high resource languages, usability of those methods on low-resource languages is unknown. In this paper, we evaluate the existing methods on Hindi and report our findings.

1 Introduction

Machine Translation (MT) has been a challenging task in natural language processing (NLP). In the last few years, there have been significant progress in MT due to easier accessibility to data, computation and discovery of new deep learning based MT techniques. The argument over using text only dataset for MT is limited when viewed with respect to how human performs translation between two languages. We, as humans comprehend the world and perform action by combining different input modalities (e.g, Text, Image etc). Similarly the same argument can be used to develop machines that can process different input modalities to perform downstream tasks. In this paper we specifically focus on the task of MT combined with visual inputs. We call this task as Multimodal MT (w.r.t the fact that we use visual modalities combined with classical text-only MT framework). We specifically aim to address the translation task between English and a low resource language (Hindi) and illustrate that by combining classical MT methods with visual information and explore how this could improve the task of translation. There are technical motivation too for performing multimodal translation tasks. Text-based systems are unable to translate sentences that are ambiguous, which can have different target translations depending upon the situation. While words surrounding the ambiguous word can clear ambiguity up to some extent, it might be helpful to introduce related information from other modalities. Following these motivation, we describe several baseline approaches well known in the field of multimodal MT and adapt them for a low-resource language. Specifically, we focus on applying the benchmark methodologies for translating between English and Hindi and vice-versa with the help of visual information.

2 Related Work

Several systems attempted to use extra information to translate text. Unimodal systems include document-level NMT, (Wang et al., 2017) which utilises document as context, sentence-level NMT with contextual information (Gain et al., 2021b), etc. Among multimodal systems, (Huang et al., 2016) used an object detection system to extract local and global image features. Thereafter, they used those image features as additional inputs to encoder and decoder. (Delbrouck and Dupont, 2017) used attention mechanism on visual inputs for the source hidden states. (Lin et al., 2020) used Dynamic Context-guided Capsule Network (Sabour et al., 2017) (DCCN) for iterative extraction of related visual features. Su et al. (2018) demonstrated an unsupervised method based on the language translation cycle consistency loss conditioned on

Proceedings of the First Workshop on Multimodal Machine Translation for Low Resource Languages (MMTLRL 2021), in conjuction with RANLP-2021, September 7, 2021. pages 40–44
https://doi.org/10.26615/978-954-452-073-1_007

Figure 1: An example of the multimodal dataset

the image. This is done to learn the bidirectional multi-modal translation simultaneously. Moreover, Su et al. (2021) showed that jointly learning text-image interaction instead of modeling them separately using attention networks is more useful.

There exists a few multimodal Machine Translation (MMT) methods for English-Hindi language pair. (Gupta et al., 2021) proposed to enhance the textual input by bringing the visual information to a textual domain by extracting object tags from the image. For pre-training, they used IIT corpus (Kunchukuttan et al., 2018). Other methods include usage of doubly attentive decoders as mentioned in Section 4.2.

3 Dataset Description & Pre-processing

We use Hindi Visual Genome 1.1 dataset (Nakazawa et al., 2021) introduced in The 8-th Workshop on Asian Translation (WAT) consisting of a total of $32,922$ sentences splited between 28929 train, 998 valid, 1595 test and 1400 challenge sentences. Each sentence represents a caption/description of a rectangular portion of an image, associated with the sentence. Coordinates of the rectangular portion is available with the dataset.

We convert all the datasets into lowercase. Then, we combine HindEnCorp (Bojar et al., 2014) and Visual Genome 1.1 training set and learn byte-pair-encoding (Sennrich et al., 2016) with $20,000$ operations using subword-nmt [1].

For image processing, we use the following two methods:

- We crop the rectangular portion of the image, which represents the caption and discard the remaining part of the image as they may not contribute much to the translation performance and can introduce noise. In our experiments in Section 5, we represent experiments with cropped image with an *crop* identifier.
- Sometimes, the cropped images are too small and can miss out important information. Also, in some cases, translation system might utilise background image information. Therefore, we perform another set of experiments with no cropping. In Section 5, absence of *crop* identifier indicate usage of full image.

We extract pre-trained ResNet50 features from the images as ResNet50 is used for image features in most of the existing methods.

4 Methods

4.1 Multimodal Transformer

We use a transformer based Multimodal Machine Translation approach proposed by (Yao and Wan, 2020), where they suggested that if every word is considered as a node, then Transformer can be regarded as a variant of Graph Neural Network (GNN) (Yao et al., 2020) which treats each sentence as a fully-connected graph with words as node.

We adapt this technique for our language pair. As described in the paper using their default configurations, we initialize word embedding by 300 dimension pre-trained GloVe word embeddings. We do not pre-train the systems. We train the systems with Visual Genome dataset (Nakazawa et al., 2021).

4.2 Doubly-Attentive Decoder

A multimodal architecture introduced by (Calixto and Liu, 2017)(Calixto et al., 2017) consists of bidirectional Recurrent Neural Network (BRNN) as encoder type, and doubly-attentive RNN as decoder type which incorporates two independent attention mechanisms, one over source language words and the other over different areas of an image. The decoder incorporates spatial visual features obtained

[1] https://github.com/rsennrich/subword-nmt

Table 1: Results obtained by different systems. BLEU is calculated using multi-bleu.perl. sBLEU_intl represents sacreBLEU with intl tokenizer

Method	Test Set				Challenge Set			
	BLEU	RIBES	sacreBLEU	sBLEU_intl	BLEU	RIBES	sacreBLEU	sBLEU_intl
Volta(Gupta et al., 2021)	44.21	0.8186	-	-	52.02	0.8541	-	-
iitp(Gain et al., 2021a)	42.47	0.8071	-	-	37.50	0.7908	-	-
CNLP-NITS(Laskar et al., 2021)	40.51	0.8032	-	-	39.28	0.7920	-	-
CNLP-NITS	39.46	0.8020	-	-	33.57	0.7541	-	-
WAT 2021 Organizer(Nakazawa et al., 2021)	38.63	0.7674	-	-	20.34	0.6442	-	-
Multimodal_Transformer(Yao and Wan, 2020)	38.30	0.7596	37.6	38.1	24.29	0.6708	23.7	24.2
Multimodal_Transformer_crop	38.53	0.7703	37.9	38.3	27.91	0.6882	27.4	27.8
NMT_src+img(Calixto et al., 2017)	39.83	0.7968	39.6	39.6	31.41	0.7387	30.8	31.3
NMT_src+img_crop	39.72	0.7910	39.6	39.6	31.81	0.7348	31.4	31.6
Transformer_text_only(Vaswani et al., 2017)	41.97	0.8091	41.9	41.9	28.53	0.6933	28.3	28.5

using pre-trained convolutional neural networks (CNNs).

There are several ways to adapt this method. (Dutta Chowdhury et al., 2018) used synthetic data for training. (Sanayai Meetei et al., 2019) used cropped rectangular portion of images to assist the system to translate. (Laskar et al., 2020) utilizes pre-train word embeddings of the monolingual corpus and additional parallel data (IITB corpus). In (Laskar et al., 2021), they made attempts to utilize phrase pairs (Sen et al., 2021) to enhance the translation performance. (Gain et al., 2021a) used a combination of systems, one with pre-training and one without pre-training for text along with cropped rectangular portions of images. We perform our experiments on $NMT_{src+img}$ method as described in (Calixto et al., 2017). For sake of better comparison with other methods, we do not pre-train the systems using additional data except for learning byte-pair-encoding described in Section 3

4.3 Text Only Transformer

We experiment on the standard transformer (Vaswani et al., 2017) model using its fairseq (Ott et al., 2019) implementation. We byte-pair-encode texts by HindEnCorp and Visual Genome 1.1 training set using fastBPE. We do not use any image features on this method.

5 Evaluation Results

For every method, we train the model with 100 epochs and pick the model with best validation set result to generate translations. We keep the same hyper-parameters as reported in the respected paper. We translate all text from English to Hindi by using beam size of 5. For BLEU and RIBES score, we tokenize all texts with Indic-tokenizer and calculate BLEU with Moses *multi-bleu.perl* and RIBES v1.02.4 [2]. We calculate BLEU scores using sacreBLEU (Post, 2018) using two different tokenizers [3]. We report our results in Table 1. First five rows contains official results from WAT 2021. Row 6-10 contain results by other methods experimented by us. For the test set, the object tag based system (Gupta et al., 2021) secured the best result with 44.21 BLEU score and 0.8186 RIBES score. It is to be noted that, results obtained using other methods are close. Even text-only system generated good results and only two systems generated better results than text-only system. Considering text-only system do not use any pre-training and other systems use sophisticated methods for pre-training, we suggest that image features have minimal impact on the test set by most of the systems.

The challenge set was created by searching for (particularly) ambiguous English words based on the embedding similarity and manually selecting those where the image and surrounding text help to resolve the ambiguity. Object tag based system performs excellently compared to the other methods and achieves 52.02 BLEU points. Most of the systems perform better than the text-only MNMT. Thus, image features have significant contribution in the performance of the challenge set. It is to be noted that, while image features add extra information to clarify ambiguous sentences, it also drops translation results in non-ambiguous sentences, acting as noise. In future, it will be important to build generalized system that can handle both of these properties.

Furthermore, we notice that cropped images helped to generate better results than that of full images.

[2] `http://lotus.kuee.kyoto-u.ac.jp/WAT/evaluation/automatic_evaluation_systems/automaticEvaluationHI.html`

[3] sacreBLEU signature is: *BLEU+case.mixed+numrefs.1+smooth.exp+tok.(13a,intl)+version.1.4.13*

6 Research Directions

Multimodal Machine Translation approach proposed by (Yao and Wan, 2020) (Multimodal Transformer) used cross-attention mechanism in place of standard self attention to model the interdependence between textual and visual modalities. Cross attention mechanism is used as a generalization of self-attention mechanism inside transformer models where the input Query (Q) is different compared to same Key (K) and Value (V) vectors. The standard mechanism used in Multimodal transformer was to input concatenated representation of textual and visual tokens as Query vector whereas visual tokens are input as both Key and Value vectors. We propose the following directions for future experiments.

- Implement cross-attention mechanism to model dependence between textual and visual representation by using different input modalities as Key and Query vector, respectively. This should be different as modeled by Multimodal transformer.
- Model text-image and image-text relationship with the help of cross-attention, by different choice of Q and K. For text-image relationship, we use Q as visual tokens and K as text tokens and vice versa for image-text relationship.
- Concatenating text-image and image-text representations as more compact measure of interdependence between the two.

We aim to do these experiments in the next iterations of the paper.

7 Conclusion

Neural machine translation is a very challenging task as one sentence can be translated into multiple ways. Multimodal translation is used to introduce information from different modalities to assist the system to translate. There are several systems that translate multimodal information from one language to the other. These methods are proven to be helpful to generate better translation on high resource languages including English, German, French, etc. However, it was unknown how useful these methods are, specifically on low resource languages like Hindi. We show comparisons of different state-of-the-art MNMT systems. We observe that multimodal information is useful to translate ambiguous sentences on Hindi. Furthermore, we found that multimodal information can act as noise and may not be worth using in case of non-ambiguous sentences. We hope those will serve as reference for future MNMT systems on low resource settings. In future, we would like to propose different MNMT methods for low resource languages maximizing multimodal information to improve translation while minimizing the same acting as noise. Furthermore, we would like to extend our work on more existing methods and adapt them to more low resource languages.

References

Ondřej Bojar, Vojtěch Diatka, Pavel Rychlý, Pavel Straňák, Vít Suchomel, Aleš Tamchyna, and Daniel Zeman. 2014. HindEnCorp - Hindi-English and Hindi-only Corpus for Machine Translation. In *Proceedings of the Ninth International Conference on Language Resources and Evaluation (LREC'14)*, Reykjavik, Iceland. European Language Resources Association (ELRA).

Iacer Calixto and Qun Liu. 2017. Incorporating global visual features into attention-based neural machine translation. In *Proceedings of the 2017 Conference on Empirical Methods in Natural Language Processing*, pages 992–1003, Copenhagen, Denmark. Association for Computational Linguistics.

Iacer Calixto, Qun Liu, and Nick Campbell. 2017. Doubly-attentive decoder for multi-modal neural machine translation. In *Proceedings of the 55th Annual Meeting of the Association for Computational Linguistics (Volume 1: Long Papers)*, pages 1913–1924, Vancouver, Canada. Association for Computational Linguistics.

Jean-Benoit Delbrouck and Stéphane Dupont. 2017. Modulating and attending the source image during encoding improves multimodal translation.

Koel Dutta Chowdhury, Mohammed Hasanuzzaman, and Qun Liu. 2018. Multimodal neural machine translation for low-resource language pairs using synthetic data. In *Proceedings of the Workshop on Deep Learning Approaches for Low-Resource NLP*, pages 33–42, Melbourne. Association for Computational Linguistics.

Baban Gain, Dibyanayan Bandyopadhyay, and Asif Ekbal. 2021a. IITP at WAT 2021: System description for English-Hindi Multimodal Translation Task. In *Proceedings of the 8th Workshop on Asian Translation (WAT2021)*, pages 161–165, Online. Association for Computational Linguistics.

Baban Gain, Rejwanul Haque, and Asif Ekbal. 2021b. Not all contexts are important: The impact of effective context in conversational neural machine translation. In *2021 International Joint Conference on Neural Networks (IJCNN)*.

Kshitij Gupta, Devansh Gautam, and Radhika Mamidi. 2021. ViTA: Visual-linguistic translation by aligning object tags. In *Proceedings of the 8th Workshop on Asian Translation (WAT2021)*, pages 166–173, Online. Association for Computational Linguistics.

Po-Yao Huang, Frederick Liu, Sz-Rung Shiang, Jean Oh, and Chris Dyer. 2016. Attention-based multimodal neural machine translation. In *Proceedings of the First Conference on Machine Translation: Volume 2, Shared Task Papers*, pages 639–645, Berlin, Germany. Association for Computational Linguistics.

Anoop Kunchukuttan, Pratik Mehta, and Pushpak Bhattacharyya. 2018. The IIT Bombay English-Hindi parallel corpus. In *Proceedings of the Eleventh International Conference on Language Resources and Evaluation (LREC 2018)*, Miyazaki, Japan. European Language Resources Association (ELRA).

Sahinur Rahman Laskar, Abdullah Faiz Ur Rahman Khilji, Darsh Kaushik, Partha Pakray, and Sivaji Bandyopadhyay. 2021. Improved English to Hindi multimodal neural machine translation. In *Proceedings of the 8th Workshop on Asian Translation (WAT2021)*, pages 155–160, Online. Association for Computational Linguistics.

Sahinur Rahman Laskar, Abdullah Faiz Ur Rahman Khilji, Partha Pakray, and Sivaji Bandyopadhyay. 2020. Multimodal neural machine translation for English to Hindi. In *Proceedings of the 7th Workshop on Asian Translation*, pages 109–113, Suzhou, China. Association for Computational Linguistics.

Huan Lin, Fandong Meng, Jinsong Su, Yongjing Yin, Zhengyuan Yang, Yubin Ge, Jie Zhou, and Jiebo Luo. 2020. Dynamic context-guided capsule network for multimodal machine translation. *Proceedings of the 28th ACM International Conference on Multimedia*.

Toshiaki Nakazawa, Hideki Nakayama, Chenchen Ding, Raj Dabre, Shohei Higashiyama, Hideya Mino, Isao Goto, Win Pa Pa, Anoop Kunchukuttan, Shantipriya Parida, Ondřej Bojar, Chenhui Chu, Akiko Eriguchi, Kaori Abe, Yusuke Oda, and Sadao Kurohashi. 2021. Overview of the 8th workshop on Asian translation. In *Proceedings of the 8th Workshop on Asian Translation (WAT2021)*, pages 1–45, Online. Association for Computational Linguistics.

Myle Ott, Sergey Edunov, Alexei Baevski, Angela Fan, Sam Gross, Nathan Ng, David Grangier, and Michael Auli. 2019. fairseq: A fast, extensible toolkit for sequence modeling. In *Proceedings of NAACL-HLT 2019: Demonstrations*.

Matt Post. 2018. A call for clarity in reporting BLEU scores. In *Proceedings of the Third Conference on Machine Translation: Research Papers*, pages 186–191, Belgium, Brussels. Association for Computational Linguistics.

Sara Sabour, Nicholas Frosst, and Geoffrey E Hinton. 2017. Dynamic routing between capsules.

Loitongbam Sanayai Meetei, Thoudam Doren Singh, and Sivaji Bandyopadhyay. 2019. WAT2019: English-Hindi translation on Hindi visual genome dataset. In *Proceedings of the 6th Workshop on Asian Translation*, pages 181–188, Hong Kong, China. Association for Computational Linguistics.

Sukanta Sen, Mohammed Hasanuzzaman, Asif Ekbal, Pushpak Bhattacharyya, and Andy Way. 2021. Neural machine translation of low-resource languages using smt phrase pair injection. *Natural Language Engineering*, 27(3):271–292.

Rico Sennrich, Barry Haddow, and Alexandra Birch. 2016. Neural machine translation of rare words with subword units. In *Proceedings of the 54th Annual Meeting of the Association for Computational Linguistics (Volume 1: Long Papers)*, pages 1715–1725, Berlin, Germany. Association for Computational Linguistics.

Jinsong Su, Jinchang Chen, Hui Jiang, Chulun Zhou, Huan Lin, Yubin Ge, Qingqiang Wu, and Yongxuan Lai. 2021. Multi-modal neural machine translation with deep semantic interactions. *Information Sciences*, 554:47–60.

Yuanhang Su, Kai Fan, Nguyen Bach, C.-C. Jay Kuo, and Fei Huang. 2018. Unsupervised multi-modal neural machine translation. *CoRR*, abs/1811.11365.

Ashish Vaswani, Noam Shazeer, Niki Parmar, Jakob Uszkoreit, Llion Jones, Aidan N Gomez, Ł ukasz Kaiser, and Illia Polosukhin. 2017. Attention is all you need. In *Advances in Neural Information Processing Systems*, volume 30. Curran Associates, Inc.

Longyue Wang, Zhaopeng Tu, Andy Way, and Qun Liu. 2017. Exploiting cross-sentence context for neural machine translation. In *Proceedings of the 2017 Conference on Empirical Methods in Natural Language Processing*, pages 2826–2831, Copenhagen, Denmark. Association for Computational Linguistics.

Shaowei Yao and Xiaojun Wan. 2020. Multimodal transformer for multimodal machine translation. In *Proceedings of the 58th Annual Meeting of the Association for Computational Linguistics*, pages 4346–4350, Online. Association for Computational Linguistics.

Shaowei Yao, Tianming Wang, and Xiaojun Wan. 2020. Heterogeneous graph transformer for graph-to-sequence learning. In *Proceedings of the 58th Annual Meeting of the Association for Computational Linguistics*, pages 7145–7154, Online. Association for Computational Linguistics.